MINDSET

How to Transform Your Life
From Ordinary to Extraordinary

James Justin

MINDSET: How to Transform Your Life from Ordinary to Extraordinary

By James Justin

ISBN-13: 978-0-9971126-5-8

Book Industry Standards and Communications (BISAC) Categories: Psychology, Self-help, Personal Growth, Success, Motivation, Inspirational

Keywords: MINDSET, Positive Thinking, Positive Mental Attitude, Success, Joy, Happiness, Happy, Motivation, Psychology, Mental toughness, Belief System, Habit, Feelings, Emotions, Emotional Intelligence, Results, Solutions, Peak Performance, Extraordinary Life, Abundance Life.

CoachJamesJustin.com
6601 Old Winter Garden Rd.
Suite 104
Orlando, FL 32835

Dedication

This book is dedicated to my wife, Dr. Lauretta Justin. Without you, I would not be who I am, and this book would not be a reality. Thank you for challenging me to think bigger. I love you, my sexy butterfly!

Contents

Introduction 1

Chapter 1. Define Your Extraordinary Life............................3

Chapter 2. Understand the Power of Your Mind 15

Chapter 3. Change Your MINDSET, Change Your Life! 37

Chapter 4. Change Your EMOTIONS, Change Your Life ...69

Chapter 5. Change Your HABIT, Change Your Life............87

Chapter 6. How to ACHIEVE Your Extraordinary Life.......103

Chapter 7. How to MAINTAIN Your Extraordinary Life 121

Conclusion 125

Notes 129

References..163

About the Author 165

Products..167

Book Description 169

Introduction

"Where your mind goes, your life follows. Therefore, if you change your MINDSET, you'll change your Life!"
James Justin

Once upon a time, a woman named Sue woke up one morning, looked in the mirror and noticed she had only three strings of hair on her head.

"Well," she said, "I think I'll braid my hair today." So she did, and she had a wonderful day.

The next day she woke up, looked in the mirror and saw that she had only two hairs on her head. "Hmmmm," she said, "I think I'll part my hair down the middle today." So she did, and she had a grand day.

The next day, Sue woke up, looked in the mirror and noticed that she had only one hair on her head.

"Well," she said, "I'm going to wear my hair in a ponytail today." So she did, and she had a fun day!

The next day she woke up, looked in the mirror and noticed that there wasn't a single hair on her head.

"YAAAY!" she exclaimed, "I don't have to fix my hair today! I can just enjoy the day!" So she did, and she had an extraordinary day!

Your perspective determines your reality. It also determines who you are. Therefore, where your mind goes, your life follows.

Sue's story illustrates the primary key to transforming your life. It's called **MINDSET**.

Your MINDSET determines your feelings, your feelings determine your actions and your actions determine your results. If you change your MINDSET, you'll change your life!

Like Sue, if you develop a positive mental attitude and pursue your goals, you'll achieve anything you desire. If you can dream it, you can achieve it!

This book is written to show you how. It features success stories from people like you who have used its principles to achieve extraordinary results!

It's not what you don't know that's limiting your success; it's what you don't know that you don't know. Your MINDSET holds the key to the abundant life.

I wrote this book to help you maximize your full potential and achieve an EXTRAORDINARY life!

Everything you need to succeed is already within you! You have the power to create the life of your dreams! You can achieve lasting success, joy and happiness! All this book does is help you *automate* it by helping you change your **THINKING**.

Chapter 1

Define Your Extraordinary Life

"An extraordinary life is a life in which you felt deep passion for everything you did, and always had time for what matters most. A life in which you had the power, the daring, and the will to make your boldest dreams come true, all while you happily left feelings of inadequacy or guilt behind."
Jessica DiLullo Herrin

Have you ever wondered what life would look like if your life was completely transformed? If you were living life on *your* terms. And if you were living your God-given life rather than living for people?

How would it FEEL to know that you're running at your optimum level and achieving extraordinary results?

• You'd be happier!

• You'd be healthier!

• You'd be wealthier!

• You'd have healthier relationships!

• You'd enjoy your life to the fullest, right?

3

Now, close your eyes and imagine that you're enjoying your extraordinary life...

- What are you seeing?

- What are you doing?

- What are you **FEELING**?

Take a moment to reflect and meditate on the life you want. Visualize the life of your dreams. Imagine yourself achieving and enjoying your ideal life!

Repeat this exercise as often as needed! It is designed to help you visualize where you want to go. Once you have a mental image of your extraordinary life, write it down. You can even draw it as well!

Defining Your Extraordinary Life

What's an extraordinary life? It's different for each person. That's why I recommend that you take some time to reflect, and then write down your own definition. This chapter offers powerful guidelines to help you define your own ideal life.

There are many ways to define an extraordinary life. We all have the choice and the power to create lifestyle we desire. For some people, it's about physical health. For others, it's developing relationships.

Also, some people believe the "good life" is all about having...

...Fast cars...Yachts...Beach-front houses...Olympic-size pools...Fancy restaurants...Fancy drinks...Long, curving driveways...Private jets...Travel...Building an empire at all cost!

Basically, their lives reflect an episode of the "Lifestyles of the Rich and Famous" television show. For others, "the good life" includes meeting the basic human needs such food, air, clothing and shelter and safety.

With my family, we have defined an extraordinary life based on the following five core values:

The Justin's Core Values Chart

> **Faith and spirituality**

> **Family and friends**

> **Fitness and health**

> **Finance and charity**

> **Fun and leisure**

5 Areas of Mastery to Create an Extraordinary Life

"Ultimately, an extraordinary life means life on your terms. But no matter how you define what a truly magnificent life is, there are two skills you must master: the science of achievement, and the art of fulfillment."
Tony Robins

In the process of creating the life of your dreams, there are five core areas that I recommend you focus on:

1. Spiritual Health: This area focuses on gaining self-knowledge, awareness and discovering your ultimate potential, purpose, passion and goals. For me, spiritual health is about developing a personal relationship with God. Your spiritual health is where your belief system is established and continues to grow. Faith plays a major role in living the life of your dreams. Faith gives you clarity, certainty and balance in life.

2. Psychological Health: It's your well-being that encompasses the mental, emotional, and behavioral dimensions of your general health.

Your **mental health** is the "thinking" component of psychological health that allows you to accurately perceive reality, and respond rationally and effectively.

Your **emotional health** is the subjective side of psychological health, and includes your feelings and moods. Your emotional intelligence is your ability to accurately assess, monitor and manage your emotions. While you cannot control people's emotions, you can manage your response to their emotional triggers and behaviors.

Your **behavioral health** is determined by the habits you practice daily.

Developing and practicing positive psychological health is one the best steps toward an extraordinary life. When you develop your mind, you position yourself to attract all that is good.

Your MINDSET determines your feelings; your feelings determine your actions and your actions determine your results. To change your result, change what goes into your mind and take a positive step each day toward your goal.

**When you develop your mind,
you position yourself to attract all that is good.**

3. Physical Health: It's critical for overall well-being, and the most visible of the various dimensions of health, including intellectual, emotional, behavioral, social and environmental health. Some of the most obvious signs that we are unhealthy appear on our bodies. You cannot be successful without good health.

It's devastating to see so many people suffering from various disorders and diseases such as bipolar, anxiety, diabetes, heart problems and cancer. Follow your doctor's recommendation to obtain and maintain good health.

4. Relational Health: A healthy relationship with family, friends and others is essential to your success. As I often preach: Success is a team sport, and there's no "I" in team. If you want to achieve a life of unlimited abundance, you need a clear goal, an effective strategy and a healthy team.

Family, friends and peers can be the members of your natural support. Whereas, a life coach or a counselor can the professional member of your team. The key is to develop healthy relationship with people who can help you achieve your goals while you're helping them as well. For details on how to develop healthy relationship, you can get started by reading my book **"7 Steps to Develop Healthy Relationships with Anyone."**

In your efforts toward healthy relationships, I urge you to spend quality time with your loved ones. Spend time playing and enjoying each other; don't make excuses around not having time. This is your LIFE! You must find time for your family in spite of everything else. There is no escape. The quality time you invest building relationship with your family and friends has tremendous impact on your well-being and success. It's a great form of return on investment.

5. Financial Health: Working and playing gives us balance in life. More importantly, when you work and invest your time, money and energy, you can expect greater wealth in your life. Take time to develop and enjoy your job or your business!

Financial health is a state of mind. It's not just about money. It's about the quality of life you enjoy with your loved ones. It's about GIVING back and helping others. "You can get everything in life you want; if you will just help enough other people get what they want" (Zig Ziglar). For more information on how to achieve financial health, read my book **"12 Steps to Achieve Financial Freedom."**

As you continue to practice these areas of mastery, you'll develop work-life balance. They will guide you in achieving your goals and finding fulfillment.

Why Define Your Ideal Lifestyle?

It's critical to your success, joy and fulfillment to describe the life of your dreams. If you don't know what you want, how can you ever achieve it?

If you don't know where you want to go, how can you ever get there? And if you don't define the life you want, someone else will define it for you.

In the words of Lewis Carroll, "If you don't know where you are going, any road will get you there."

If you don't define the life you want, someone else will!

To achieve your extraordinary life, you must take the first step: You must **define** it!

The process of defining the life you want is an important step to accomplish yours goals. It's also much easier to communicate your dreams and goals when they are written down.

When writing down the life you want, write it with simple, concise language! *"Write the vision, and make it plain"* (Habakkuk 2:2). When your goals are clearly defined, it's easier for your team to help you achieve them.

How to define your extraordinary life

Defining the life of your dreams is a process. Start where you are now and update your goals as you go forward. Here are three tips to get started:

1. Get clarity

Prayer and meditate are great ways to find clarity and direction for your life. Finding clarity to define your goals will help you save time and money. You'll also be energized to pursue your goals with passion and fulfillment when you have clarity.

2. Write down the life of your dream in plain language

Imagine the life you want and write it down. You don't have to wait until you have a perfect mission, vision and purpose statement to transform your life. You can start with a brief description of your goals and update it later.

When you write your vision, do so in plain language. It's easier to communicate. It's easier for your team to follow and help you achieve it.

3. Get help

Defining your ideal life doesn't have to be done alone, you can get professional help. Your team members such as a professional life coach or a psychotherapist can help you identify your extraordinary life; and formulate a plan to achieve it.

Your friends and family can also be helpful since they know you very well. For example, my wife and I worked together to develop our ideal lifestyle. We even got our children involved in the process.

We started by defining our family core values. We review them as needed. More importantly, we developed a *plan* to achieve the life we want.

In addition to the previous tips, I also enjoy meditating on the following quotes:

"Be transformed by the renewing of your MIND..."
Romans 12:2, TLV

"An extraordinary life is a state of mind. It's the beauty of enjoying everyday life."
James Justin

"The extraordinary life is the fullness of love, joy, peace, patience, kindness, goodness, faithfulness, gentleness, and self-control."
Galatians 5:22-23

"For I know the plans I have for you, declares the Lord, plans for welfare and not for evil, to give you a future and a hope."
Jeremiah 29:11, ESV

"I can do all things through Christ who strengthens me. And my God shall supply all your needs according to His riches in glory by Christ Jesus."
Philippians 4:13 and Philippians 4:19

The Abundant Life Prayer

"Today, I live in abundance in my Spirit, Soul, Body; and every area of my life!

Everything and everyone I need to create my abundance life come to me today in effortless ease! For it is God's pleasure to lavish his blessings over me!

As a result, I'm abundantly blessed; and everyone that comes in contact with me shall also be blessed!"
Dr. Lauretta Justin

These quotes give me inspiration, clarity and direction for my life. And I believe they can guide you as well! I encourage you to take a minute each day to pray and meditate on the life of your dreams; and take one action per day toward your goals. When you pray, believe that you are achieving goals. As noted in the book of Mark 11:24, *"Therefore I say to you, whatever things you ask when you pray, believe that you receive them, and you will have them."*

Chapter 2

Understand the Power
of Your Mind

"For as he thinks in his heart, so is he."
King Solomon

I n 2006, many people, including myself, read and watched Rhonda Byrne's book and DVD series, "The Secret!" This personal development volume was highly endorsed by many, including television icon Oprah Winfrey. "The Secret" introduced readers to the **law of attraction** and its impact on our thinking, our feelings, our actions and our results. It showed readers how to release the power of their minds through the law of attraction.

In pursuing the life of your dreams, it's important to understand the power of your mind and how your mind works. This is important because your mind determines your feelings, your feelings determine your actions and your actions determine your results.

As you continue to understand the power of your mind, you'll be able to use it to transform your life and to attract the life of your dreams.

The Law of Attraction: How to Attract What You Want and Not What You Don't Want

The life of your dreams awaits you! Now is the time to position yourself to attract your ideal life. Are you ready to get started?

The law of attraction is a way to describe the principle of like attracts like. In New Thought philosophy, it's used to sum up the idea that by focusing on positive or negative thoughts, a person invites those positive and negative experiences into their life. Our results are reflections of our thinking.

The law of attraction suggests that we have the power to transform our lives by attracting whatsoever we focus on and commit to.

3 Steps to Practice the Law of Attraction

The law of attraction promotes three simple steps to transform your life and achieve your goals.

Step 1. Ask for what you want. In essence, it's important to clearly define your desires, and do not limit yourself to any possibility and pursue your goals.

Step 2. Believe in your dreams. Act, speak and think as though you have already received what you've asked for. When you radiate the aura of having received your desires, the Law of Attraction moves people, events and circumstances for you to receive your desires.

Step 3. Imagine your dreams. Feel the way you will feel when your dreams come true. Feeling good now, puts you on the frequency of what you want. That type of feeling compels you to take actions to achieve your goals.

The Real Secret of the Law of Attraction

As a student of faith, I believe in the Law of Attraction. I believe that our faith is an important part of our success. And wherever our minds go, our life will follow.

Most people who have achieved lasting success believed in their dreams and pursued their goals. They have a disciplined focus on their vision, mission, purpose and passion. They create a winning strategy, and they develop a winning team to help them achieve their goals. More importantly, successful people take actions to achieve the life of their goals! As noted by Walt Disney, "If you can dream it, you can do it. All our dreams can come true if we have the courage to pursue them."

Pray for your dreams and goals, and believe that you are empowered to achieve them!

The law of attraction teaches us to believe, pursue and achieve our dreams. In your prayers, be sure to pray for your dreams and goals, and believe that you are empowered to achieve them! Jesus said, *"Keep on asking, and you will receive what you ask for. Keep on seeking, and you will find. Keep on knocking, and the door will be opened to you. For everyone who asks, receives. Everyone who seeks, finds. And to everyone who knocks, the door will be opened" (Matthew 7:7-8).*

Faith is a major key in achieving your full potential and achieving lasting success, joy and happiness. Faith builds your self-esteem and shapes your decisions. Your faith will affect your feelings and your actions. I believe that 80 percent of your actions are driven by your beliefs.

What is faith?

"Faith shows the reality of what we hope for; it is the evidence of things we cannot see. Through their faith, the people in days of old earned a good reputation. By faith we understand that the entire universe was formed at God's command, that what we now see did not come from anything that can be seen" (Hebrews 11:1-3). Your faith is shaped primarily by your belief system. Your beliefs impact your thinking, feeling, actions and results.

> *"The power of your mind is activated by your faith.*
> *Whatsoever you believe, you can achieve."*
> **James Justin**

5 Steps to Activate the Law of Attraction in Your Life

Step 1: Decision
Pick a specific goal that is consistent with your interests, faith, capability and resources; and write it down in plain English! Research reveals that people who clearly define their goals are more likely to accomplish them. Here are two examples:

I am celebrating feeling light and alive at my perfect body weight of 200 lbs. by December 31st!

I am saving $100 per month for my emergency fund.

To remain focused on your goals, affirm what you want. Avoid spending time and energy on what you **don't** want.

Here are some positive affirmations to meditate on and to keep your mind focused:

Thank you, God, for this wonderful day! I am healthier than ever!

I'm wealthier than ever before… I'm happy to be able to save and invest my money and time wisely!

I am attracting joy into my life!

I am confidently expressing myself openly and honestly!

I am effectively communicating my needs and desires to my loved ones and to other people!

19

I am feeling relaxed and grateful to be alive!

Step 2: Imagine
Create a clear picture of what you want, real and positive impact on your life and on the world and commit to achieve it. Visualize yourself achieving your goal now. What are you seeing? Write it down!

What are you feeling? Write it down! What would you be doing? Write it down and become one with your goal until you achieve it! This process will help you remain focused on your goals.

Step 3: Commitment
Take one action per day toward your goal. Without commitment, there is no accomplishment.

Step 4: Teamwork
Success is a team sport. Therefore, enlist the help of your team to accomplish your goals. As noted by Michael Jordan, *"Talent wins games, but teamwork and intelligence wins championships."*

Step 5: Celebration
Decide the benefits you'll enjoy for achieving each goal, and celebrate each win with your loved ones and your team. Peter Bondra once said, *"Celebration is a moment when the excitement of your goal makes you react to the moment."* Make your celebration fun. Have a party or take a day off! I like to go on vacation with my wife to celebrate an achieved goal.

How the Mind Works

Many people commonly confuse **brain power** with **mind power**. However, these are two separate concepts. Brain power is what we use in our daily lives to complete tasks such as breathing, eating, sleeping and working.

The **brain** is a part of the human anatomy, a very real and tangible organ. As defined by Merriam-Webster, "the brain is the organ of the body in the head that controls functions, movements, sensations, and thoughts."

The **mind** is also very real, but it is intangible, making the possibility of its power even greater. It's like a computer. In the proceeding section, we will discover how the human mind works. We'll be using triangle, iceberg and computer for our illustrations.

In psychology, the mind is the essence of a person, or the characteristic of human beings that enable them to perceive the world. It's the faculty of **consciousness**, **subconsciousness** and **unconsciousness**.

Your mind creates your reality. *"Our life is the creation of our mind" (Buddha)*. That's why I say, if you change the way you think, you'll transform your life!

The 3 Levels of the Human Mind

To better understand the power of the human mind, psychologists have divided the mind into three levels:

The **Conscious** Mind

The **Subconscious** Mind

The **Unconscious** Mind

The Human Mind Triangle

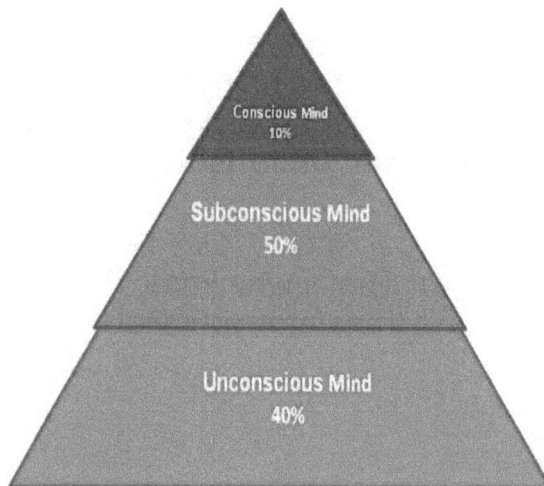

Conscious Mind
10%

Subconscious Mind
50%

Unconscious Mind
40%

The human mind is the element that enables us to be aware of ourselves and the world around us; it helps us to experience life to the fullest; to think, to feel and to act a certain way.

Imagine the very tip of a triangle as your **conscious** mind. It occupies only a small portion of space at the top. And much like an iceberg, where only a fraction of it appears above the water, your **conscious** mind consumes only about 10 percent of your mental capacity. This tip of the triangle represents the *logical* part of the mind.

Below the tip on the triangle is a slightly larger section, which Freud called the **subconscious** mind. Freud also referred to it as the preconscious mind. It is much larger than the conscious mind, and accounts for at least half of your mental capabilities. The **subconscious** is the *emotional* part of the mind.

The section of the triangle below the subconscious is called the **unconscious** mind. It occupies the remaining 30-40 percent of the triangle. It is vast and deep and largely inaccessible to conscious thought; a bit like the dark depths of the ocean.

How the 3 Tiers of the Mind Work Together

The idea of the three tiers of the human mind isn't new. Thought leaders, theologians, philosophers and psychologists such as King Solomon, St. Paul and Pierre Janet wrote extensively on MINDSET and how the mind works. However, Sigmund Freud, the famous Austrian psychologist, popularized it as we know it today.

Freud used an iceberg to illustrate how the human mind works.

The Human Mind Iceberg Model

The mind exists to help us enjoy life to the fullest by avoiding pain and embracing pleasure.

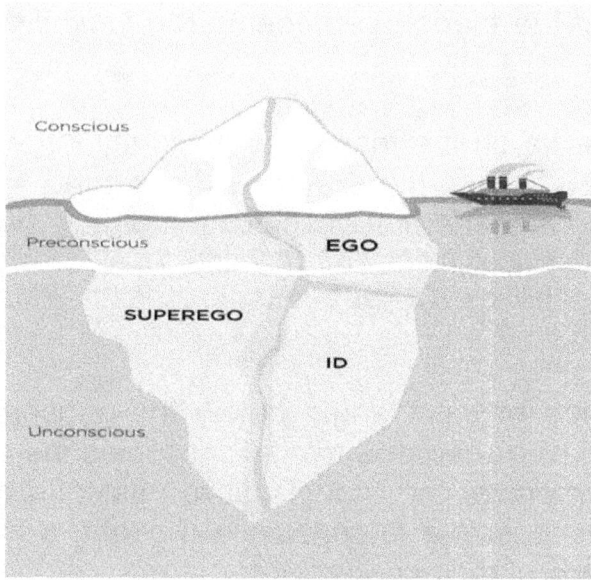

How the Mind Works

Conscious Mind Controls:
- Always available & accessible information
- Willpower
- Decision Making
- Thinking Logically

Subconscious Mind Controls:
- Data you have to dig to access
- Reoccurring thoughts
- Behaviors, habits & feelings
- Recent memories

Unconscious Mind Controls:
- Memories, Beliefs & Habits from age 0 - 7
- Traumatic Stored Events
- Phobias & Addictions
- Information that's kept hidden, locked & resists change
- Overriding information stored in other two areas
- You & Your Life

24

Your **conscious** mind is what most people associate with who you are, because it is in this part of the mind where most people live day to day. But it's by no means where all the action takes place.

Your conscious mind operates similar to a ship captain standing on the bridge barking out orders. In reality, it's the "crew" in the engine room below deck (the subconscious and the deeper unconscious) that execute the orders. The captain may command the ship, but the crew actually guides the ship, all according to what training they had been given over the years.

The **conscious** mind communicates to the outside world and the inner self through speech, pictures, writing, physical movement and thought.

On the other hand, the subconscious mind oversees our recent memories, and is in continuous contact with the resources of the unconscious mind.

The **unconscious** mind is the storehouse of all memories and past experiences, both those that have been repressed through trauma, as well as those memories that have simply been consciously forgotten and deemed no longer important to us. It's from these memories and experiences that our beliefs, habits and behaviors are formed.

The unconscious mind constantly communicates with the conscious mind via our subconscious, and is what provides us with the meaning to all our interactions with the world, as filtered through our beliefs and habits. It communicates through feelings, emotions, imagination, sensations and dreams.

A computer system is a great way to better understand how the human mind works.

Your **conscious** mind is represented by the keyboard and the monitor. Data is transmitted via the keyboard to the monitor screen. That is how your conscious mind works: Information is received via external or internal stimulus from your environment, and the results are instantly transmitted to your consciousness.

The two most powerful functions of your conscious mind:

   • **It directs your focus.**

   • **It enables you to imagine that which is not real.**

Your **subconscious** mind has a much stronger sense of awareness of your surroundings than your conscious mind. Some scientists suggest it's where the "sixth sense" originates. It is always switched on, even when you're asleep. Its sole function is to obey orders from your conscious mind.

Therefore, it's important to speak what you want, and do not focus on what you **don't** want. For example, if you want to lose 10 pounds, tell yourself that you are losing 10 pounds, instead of saying, "I don't think I can do it," or "I *may* be interested in losing 10 pounds." In my opinion, "maybe" goals hardly ever become a reality.

If you continuously focus your conscious thoughts on negativity, then your subconscious mind will obediently deliver the feelings, emotions and memories that are associated with that thinking.

For example, when you are lying in bed and hear something go "bump" in the night. If you let your thoughts and imagination wander to all the horrible things that might happen, your subconscious will expose the feelings, emotions and memories of past events that you've associated with that thought. It's the way your subconscious protects and prepares you for fight or flight behaviors.

In contrast, if you consciously direct your focus to more rational, calming thoughts, the feelings will then subside or disappear.

Some people find it quite easy and natural to develop a positive mental attitude. They can direct their thoughts toward a positive outlook on life. I want to note that it doesn't mean that they are supermen or superwomen. It simply means that they have more practice developing their positivity muscles.

> *"It's not what happens to us that break us; it's our actions to what happens to us that make us."*
> **James Justin**

It really depends on the type of programming your subconscious and unconscious have had since birth. For example, do you sway toward pessimism or optimism; negative thinking or positive thinking; happiness or depression; anger or calm; or somewhere in between?

Identify which thoughts and feelings dominate your life, and then develop a plan for improvement.

Your professional life coach or counselor can help you develop a better, more productive mental attitude.

This ability of your conscious mind to direct your attention and process everyday events is powerful. The fact that you can learn, direct your thoughts and recall information logically means that you can also *un*learn old and outdated information that you don't want to keep. This means that you can change your MINDSET to change your life!

The actual skill of directing your focus is quite simple:

1. **Make a choice** to think positive

2. **Decide how you will think** and what thoughts you will allow into your mind.

3. **Get help** from someone who's qualified to help you take action that brings you favorable results.

Our thoughts are the only true freedom that we can actually control. You cannot control what people do, but you can control your reaction by monitoring your thinking and your attitude.

A man can be physically trapped in prison, in absolute inhumane conditions, and yet still be "free" in his own mind. Dr. Victor Frankl, Nelson Mandela and others of their ilk are testament to that fact.

We alone can choose how we are going to respond to our experiences in life. God has given us free will. We *can* choose how we respond to what happens to us in life.

Your **subconscious** mind is like the random-access memory (RAM) of a computer. This part of your mind represents your short-term memories. The RAM is a type of computer memory that can be accessed randomly; that is, any byte of memory in that computer can be accessed without touching the preceding bytes. RAM is the most common type of memory found in computers and other digital devices, such as tablets, smart phones and printers.

Your **subconscious** mind is responsible to maintain any recent memories available for quicker recall when needed, such as your telephone number or the name of a person you just met. It also holds the current "programs" you run every day, such as recurring thoughts, behavior patterns, habits and feelings.

Your **unconscious** mind, however, is like the hard-disk drive in your computer. It is the long-term storage place for all your memories and "programs" installed since birth. All the memories (good and bad), experiences and data you received from the world are kept in your unconscious mind.

Ultimately, your subconscious mind uses the memories and programs stored in your unconscious mind to make sense of the world, to keep you safe, and to ensure your survival.

The logic of how your mind works is that if you survived a past experience, then your mind will help you get through similar situations by the same means, no matter how misguided, painful and unhelpful the results may actually be to you.

However, eighty percent (80%) of our decisions are based on memories and programming conditioned as a child. That's why I recommend that you keep on renewing your mind with new information and guidance that supports the life of your dreams.

For example, my parents used to tell me not to talk to strangers as a child for my own safety. However, as an adult, I automatically transferred such mindset and behavior in my life. For no obvious reason, I did not trust people. As a result, I had a hard time making new friends.

It wasn't until I received professional coaching that I realized my limiting belief about relationship was preventing me from making friends. My success coach helped me reframe my limiting belief about friendship, and develop healthier relationships. Now, I teach people how to develop healthy relationship with anyone.

Is limiting belief holding you back from achieving the life of your dreams? If so, I recommend that you get a professional coach or a counselor to help you. Life is too short to let any obstacle preventing your success. Get the help you need to achieve your goals.

How to Maximize the Power of Your Mind

"Logic will get you from A to B.
Imagination will take you everywhere."
Albert Einstein

Imagination

To maximize the power of the mind, my clients and I utilize imagination, visualization, prayer and taking actions. I also recommend that you practice these principles to unlock the power of your mind and achieve extraordinary results.

The power of your mind is unlimited. If you can imagine it and commit to it, you can achieve anything. Scientists continue to discover new functions of our minds.

Your conscious mind has the miraculous ability to imagine.

Your mind can literally imagine something that is totally new, unique and something you've never previously experienced. This is powerful, because if you can dream it and commit to it, you can achieve anything you want!

By contrast, your subconscious mind can only offer versions of what memories it has stored from your past experiences.

The really neat "trick" is that the subconscious mind can't distinguish between that which the conscious mind imagines, and that which is real. So, whatever is recalled by conscious imagination and intently focused on, also

31

recalls all the emotions and feelings associated with that image in your mind for you to experience.

**Imagination is truly a marvelous gift
we have, and one we can master
toward achieving our greatness!**

For instance, if you've ever daydreamed about winning the lottery, or perhaps looked forward to being with that someone special you love, then you would have felt the joy that those thoughts had conjured up in your head, even though you knew, intellectually, it wasn't physically happening at that very moment.

Your subconscious mind "believed" that it was happening to you, so it supplied you with the feelings and emotions it associated with those thoughts. It truly is a marvelous gift we have, and one we can master toward achieving our greatness!

Visualization

"Visualization is daydreaming with a purpose."
Robert "Bo" Bennett

In addition to imagination, visualization is a great way to begin attracting the life of your dreams. Visualization is the process of creating mental visual images of your desires. It can be used to create amazing results. For example, in one sporting study, three groups of players were tested on their ability to improve their basketball free throw accuracy. They were tested and scored at the start of the experiment, and at the end.

One group was instructed to physically practice free throws for 20 continuous days. The second group was not allowed to train at all. The third group spent 20 minutes a day getting into a relaxed state and only *imagining* themselves performing the free throws. This group was also taught that if they missed a shot in their minds, to adjust slightly and see themselves making it the next time.

At the end of the experiment the results were incredible. The group that physically practiced each day improved their score by 24%. The second group–the group that didn't practice–as expected, didn't improve at all. But the third group—the group that only visualized practicing their free throws—actually improved their score by an amazing 23%; nearly as much as the group that practiced every single day! DO NOT under estimate the power of the conscious mind!

Prayer

*"Prayer is an expression of faith;
it's as breathing is of life."*
Jonathan Edwards

Along with visualization, prayer plays a critical role in personal growth and releasing the power of your mind.

The Benefits of Prayer

According to a recent Pew Research Poll, over half of Americans pray every day. Another poll revealed that more than 75% of Americans believe that prayer is an important part of daily life. Other polls indicate that even some atheists and religiously unaffiliated individuals admit that they sometimes pray.

Social psychologist Dr. Clay Routledge noted three scientifically-supported benefits of prayer.

1. Prayer improves health by offsetting the negative effects of stress.
Researchers found that people who prayed for others were less vulnerable to the negative physical health effects stress.

2. Prayer improves self-control.
Recent research indicates that prayer can help you get more out of your "self-control muscle."

3. Prayer increases trust.

Recent studies found that having people pray together with a close friend increased feelings of unity and trust.

Prayer is a heartfelt desire that allows you to connect your thought, emotion and action toward a desired result.

Prayer works…if you know how to pray effectively.

The power of prayer is activated by faith. This means that if you're praying for a goal, believe that you're achieving it, commit to it by taking the necessary actions, and you'll achieve it. *"I tell you, you can pray for anything, and if you believe that you've received it, it will be yours" (Mark 11:24).*

Prayer is my favorite strategy for impressing a desire into my subconscious mind. Prayer is a form of communication for spiritual, psychological and physical health. It helps me eliminate unnecessary stress and to remain focused on my goals. It allows me to develop healthy relationship with God.

Prayer is an expression of desire. King David wrote, *"Delight yourself in the Lord, and He will give you the desires of your heart."* Prayer is a heartfelt expression between two beings. It is an honest conversation between you and God. Prayer can help you connect your thoughts and your feelings, and empower you to achieve the desire of your heart.

To discover the benefits of prayer, read **"The Power of Prayer,"** one of the books that Dr. Lauretta Justin and I recently published. This book is available at CoachJamesJustin.com and Amazon.

Actions

The best way to maximize the power of your mind is to take one action per day toward your goals. Without effective actions, you will not be able to achieve anything. In chapter 6, we'll discuss goal setting and how to achieve an extraordinary life.

Chapter 3

Change Your MINDSET, Change Your Life!

"Transform your life by renewing your mind."
Saint Paul

I s your MIND arranged to attract the life of your dreams? The following story illustrates the kind of MINDSET that attracts lasting success, joy and happiness...

The Story of John

John was 92 years old and blind, but he was just as sharp as he could be when his wife, Eleanor, went to heaven. He didn't feel he should live alone, so John decided to move into a nice seniors' home.

As was his habit, John arrived early on his scheduled move-in day, and waited more than an hour before a young aide named Miranda came to show him to his new room.

As John maneuvered his walker through the hallways, Miranda described his room in detail...how the sunlight came in through a big window, and there was a comfortable couch and a nice desk area...

John interrupted her and said, "I love it! I love it! I love it!" Miranda laughed and said, "Sir, we're not even there yet."

John said, "No, you don't have to show it to me for me to know that whether I like my room or not doesn't depend on how the furniture is arranged. It depends on how my mind is arranged."

Your life transformation begins in the mind. Therefore, if you change your MINDSET, you'll change your life!

Have you ever asked yourself any of these questions?

• Why is one person so motivated to achieve all kinds of success, while another feels stuck and achieves nothing?

• Why is one person sad and depressed, while another person has the fullness of joy and happiness?

• Why does one person get sick often, while another has the fullness of health?

• Why is it that while one of two people with the same background, knowledge, skills, abilities, capabilities and opportunities stays poor, while the other becomes wealthy?

• Why is one person fearful and anxious, while another is filled with faith and confidence?

• Why are some people happily married, while others struggle to maintain their marriage?

• Why is one person succeeding in life and in business, while another continues to fail personally and professionally?

Is there a common answer to these questions? The answer is YES! It's called **MINDSET**.

Your MINDSET will influence every area of your life. It will even affect whether you achieve and retain an extraordinary life.

The way you think and the way you act will determine your results. That is why even a small improvement in personal development will make a huge difference in your life experience.

Virtually, everyone who has achieved lasting success, joy and happiness adopted a growth MINDSET. John's positive mental attitude kept him centered, and that was his secret to obtain and maintain the life of his dreams!

Likewise, your breakthrough in life and in business begins in your mind. I encourage you to start developing a growth MINDSET that attracts success into your life!

In this chapter, I'll share the major principles you need to change your thinking and to change your life.

- What is MINDSET?

- What is the difference between **Fixed** and **Growth** MINDSET?

- 5 Steps to Change your MINDSET

What is MINDSET?

It's a particular way of thinking. It's a mental attitude shaped by our beliefs. I called it the mental operating system that drives our actions and results.

Your MINDSET determines your feelings; your feelings determine your actions, and your actions determine your results. If you change your MINDSET, you'll change your life!

Our MINDSET is influenced by both nature and nurture. For example, our nature determines our biological makeup, such as DNA programming, gender, skin color and height. The aspects of the environmental influences on our MINDSETs include where we live, schools we attend and the friends we have.

Dr. Lauretta Justin said, *"When we combine our nature and nurture, we get certain voices; and these voices create our MINDSETs."* There are three voices influencing our MINDSET:

- The voice of authority

- The voice of our peers

40

- The voice of our perceptions or beliefs

If you want to change your results, you must start by reframing your limiting beliefs. We'll discuss limiting beliefs later.

One of my favorite books on MINDSET is written by world-renowned Stanford University psychologist Dr. Carol Dweck. After decades of research on motivation, achievement and success, Dr. Dweck revealed the truly groundbreaking idea that MINDSET was the determining factor separating those who succeed in life and in business, from those who don't.

In her book, "MINDSET: The New Psychology of Success," Dweck reveals how success in school, work, sports, the arts and almost every area of human endeavor can be dramatically influenced by how we approach our goals.

Her research revealed the two primary MINDSETS that drive our life: the **fixed** MINDSET, and the **growth** MINDSET.

People with a fixed MINDSET believe that their basic intelligence, talents and abilities are fixed and unchangeable.

Essentially, they believe that their lives cannot be changed.

They are far less likely to flourish than those with a growth MINDSET.

Growth MINDSET people believe that their lives can be changed with new learning, strategies and commitment. They believe that their intelligence, abilities and talents are simply the starting point to the life of their dreams.

In her book, Dweck reveals how great parents, teachers, managers, and athletes can use the growth MINDSET concept to foster extraordinary results.

Fixed MINDSET

"No one is exempt from the reality of life. I was born blind, but I chose not to live in negativity; and that's my key to success and happiness."
James Justin

Do you have the fixed MINDSET, or the growth MINDSET? Before you answer this question, read the parable below and complete the Justin's MINDSET Survey listed in the Notes section of this book.

You'll get a new perspective on the way you think! As you change your limiting beliefs, you'll be empowered to transform your life!

The Parable of the Flood

Once upon a time, there was a man named Joe who was trapped in his house during a flood. He began praying for God to rescue him. He envisioned God's hand reaching down from heaven and lifting him to safety.

With the water level starting to rise in his house, Joe's neighbor urged him to leave, and offered him a ride to safety in his pickup truck. The man yelled back, "I am waiting for God to save me," as he watched the neighbor drive off.

The man continued to pray and hold on to his vision. As the water continued to rise in his house, he had to climb to the roof. A boat came by with people heading for safe ground. They yelled at the man to grab a safety rope they threw for him, but he refused, telling them that he was waiting for God to save him.

The man continued to pray, believing with all his heart that he would be saved by God. The flood waters continued to rise. A helicopter flew by and a voice came over a loudspeaker offering to lower a ladder to rescue him. The man waved the helicopter away, shouting back that he was waiting for God to save him.

Soon after the helicopter left, the flooding water swallowed the house and swept the man away. He drowned.

When the man reached heaven, he asked God, "Why didn't you save me? I believed in you with all my heart. Why did you let me drown?"

God replied, "I sent you a pick-up truck, a boat and a helicopter, and you refused all of them. What else could I possibly do for you?"

There are opportunities all around you. The opportunity you need for your miracle is in your hand RIGHT NOW! Because you can think, you can transform your life. As you continue to develop a growth MINDSET, you'll be empowered to take the right action to transform your life.

People who adopt a fixed MINDSET...

...believe that their intelligence is fixed, with little hope for growth, instilling a desire to look smart rather than being smart. People with a fixed MINDSET avoid challenges necessary for growth

...subconsciously give up easily when life's obstacles knock at their door.

...believe that efforts are useless.

...do not welcome criticism.

...often get jealous or envy the success of others.

...live a life of fear and regret.

...view setbacks as permanent, instead of temporary defeats. This limited thinking impedes efforts toward greater achievement, success and happiness.

Growth MINDSET

Having a growth mindset means understanding that intelligence, skills and abilities can be developed and improved. A growth MINDSET is a belief that we can get smarter through hard work and practice. This means that struggling with something difficult doesn't mean you're not smart: it's a chance to grow your intelligence.

Growth MINDSET people love to learn and grow. They're willing to work hard and use new strategies to achieve their goals. They're not afraid to ask for help when it's needed.

Growth MINDSET people...

...believe that their basic traits and intelligence are dynamic, changeable, and can be developed over time with the right training and persistence. This belief leads to the desire to learn and grow. People who hold this type of MINDSET embrace challenges necessary for growth.

...are positive thinkers and lovers of learning.

...take actions toward achieving their purpose, goals and destiny.

...are willing to learn and grow every day.

...are more likely to see the cup half full rather than half empty.

...are most likely to see and create opportunities out of life challenges rather than complaining of lack of opportunities.

...often have high standards for living.

...have faith and hope for a better tomorrow.

...often have a strategy or a written plan to succeed, instead of living by chance.

...don't avert challenges, but face their problems squarely, seeking solutions to overcome them. They are likely to learn lessons from their problems and turn their setbacks into comebacks.

Virtually, everyone who has achieved lasting success, adopted the growth MINDSET.

Likewise, if you want to transform your life and achieve extraordinary results, I recommend that you develop your growth MINDSET.

It's okay if you have adopted a negative mental attitude. We all have at some point. However, you cannot live in a constant state of negativity if you want a positive life.

If you want extraordinary results in life, you must develop a **positive** mental attitude and remain committed to your goals.

I know from professional experience that if you change your MINDSET and pursue your goals, you WILL change your life.

Here are some examples of people like you who have transformed their lives by renewing their MIND…

The Story of *My* Life

"I believe that all things are possible to those who believe and remain committed to their goals."
James Justin

Is life handing you a bowl of lemons? Let's turn it into sweet lemonade!

Since life is a learning field, nobody is exempt from its harsh realities. I've had my own challenges as well.

Imagine turning 16 years old, and all your friends are getting their driving permits, and venturing on their path of independence.

They begin dating, partying and planning for college.

When you applied for your driver's permit, you are quickly turned away and told, *"You'll never get a driver's license. You're legally blind. You can only see 10 percent of what everyone else sees. You don't have enough vision to drive."*

What would *you* think...what would *you* feel...and what would *you* do?

My first thoughts were, "Great; my life is over. And of course, college is definitely now out of the picture."

This isn't a tale I made up; this is the story of **my life!**

As I was trying to mentally and emotionally digest this news of blindness and its potential impact on my entire life, I experienced the full gamut of emotions. I felt shock, disappointment, anger, depression, frustration…and reeling from the crushing shock as my dreams of college, family and business—at least in my mind—were suddenly and cruelly snatched from my clutches.

It took some time to accept my vision disability. I received continuous, embracing love and support from my family and friends. I also had professional counselors and mentors who helped me along the way.

In the process of learning to overcome my vision limitations, I discovered several lifetime lessons…

• I discovered that my life isn't determined by disability; it's determined by me! I may have lost my sight, but my vision to succeed and thrive remained intact.

• I have the power to achieve anything I put my mind to. God has given me the ability to THINK. My life can be transformed by renewing my MIND and pursue my goals.

• To achieve my goals, I must take 100 percent responsibility for my life!

During this period of inspiration and enlightenment, I realized that I was created by God for the purpose of caring, sharing, giving and LOVING! I realized that I was called to help others transform their lives!

This passion was the push to ultimately earn my master's degree, and dedicate my life to self-improvement, counseling, coaching, speaking, and helping people like you for over 20 years!

You may be wondering how I overcame vision disability and transformed my life.

Well, ultimately I changed my MINDSET!

I adopted a positive mental attitude.

More importantly, I took 100 percent responsibility for my life and pursuit my goals.

This means that I stopped feeling sorry for myself and took actions to transform my life. I stopped focusing on my disability and started focusing on my abilities.

I also had some great counselors, coaches and mentors who gave me the tools and support to overcome my vision disability.

I took the advice of great people in my life such as my parents, friends, life coaches, teachers and pastors.

With the tools and strategies I learned from my mentors and counselors, I changed my limited thinking and took actions toward my goals.

With persistent and smart work, I completed my education and worked in my field of choice. More importantly, I married the love of my life and we have three handsome boys!

The chart below summarizes some of my happy moments...

"James Justin is a loving Husband, Dad and Minister"

"He's a Speaker, Author, Psychotherapist & Life Coach!"

Known as "That Happiness Guy!"

COACH JAMES JUSTIN
THAT HAPPINESS GUY
TRANSFORM OPTIMIZE ACCELERATE

I'm grateful to every member of my team! I thank God, my loved ones and my counselors who helped me reach my goals!

Special thanks go to my wife, Dr. Lauretta Justin, who believed in me and challenged me to think bigger and pursue my dreams! Without her love and support, I wouldn't be the man I am today.

Now, I use the lessons from my story to inspire and help people like you to achieve extraordinary results. I share my story here to inspire you to pursue your goals. If I can achieve anything, so can you!

If you believe in your dream and commit to it, your life will be transformed!

Mary Vogel's Story

"I felt like I was constantly stressed and overwhelmed – like it would never go away... and it seemed like I kept finding myself in situations where I just didn't know what to do, or how to get out of them – as if I was getting in my own way. It was a never ending cycle of insecurity, self-doubts and negative thoughts... It affected EVERYTHING – at home, at work – EVERYWHERE!"

"It wasn't until I met James that my life took a huge transformation – and I began shedding all the emotional baggage, pain and struggles... Decisions began coming much easier – I even found myself politely saying no to people, and I regained complete control of my life."

"I got a better job making a lot more money, and for the first time EVER, I literally felt like I could BREATHE – and fill my lungs and heart full of oxygen and joy and happiness!! And LOVE!!"

"While working with James, EVERYTHING in my life became much brighter and much clearer! Sure – I had moments of challenges, but I didn't get STUCK there – stuck in negative emotions, bad habits, fears and irrational behavior. James helped me work right thru them! My marriage turned INCREDIBLE! Relationships blossomed! Life became much easier. I started sleeping like a

baby - all the way thru the night! James taught me HOW to get un-stuck and STAY un-stuck! And how to keep my life in motion!"

Tom Colini's Story

"I felt like I had a never-ending ton of weight on my shoulders, and it was my job to make everyone around me happy – both at work and at home. The problem was – I WASN'T HAPPY and I literally felt like I couldn't breathe… Truthfully – LIFE SUCKED… And every ounce of energy was completely drained from me… And then I met James…"

"Look…Don't make the mistake that I did. I had James' number on my desk for two years, and I dragged it out another two years before I finally called him. James is a truly amazing life changer! Get on your phone and call him or email him today by visiting CoachJamesJustin.com!

Don't let another two minutes go by, much less two years! I love this guy! Let him help you like he helped me, and believe me, if he can help me, he definitely can help you. Call him now!"

Stephanie Brown's Story

"You see, James taught me a very powerful lesson: My success AND happiness is determined by ME! It makes perfect sense to me now. I'm the one that has the responsibility, the choice and the power to transform and maximize my life to the fullest."

"James taught me the 'HOW' questions! How can I receive all God's blessings for my life? How could I get rid of everything that's holding me back? How could I have the best relationships ever, complete self-confidence, intimacy and love? How can I achieve my full potential...my ideal life...my dreams; to be the best person ever: the best wife, the best mother, the best provider? And how can I help others do the same thing?"

"This is a really cool concept, and it makes complete sense. James proved to me that it doesn't take any more effort to be happy than it does to be depressed. It's just a choice...if you know HOW to make it! Exciting, right?"

There are many counseling and coaching theories and techniques available to help people. Some of these methods are designed to analyze the *WHAT* and the *WHY...*

- What's wrong?

- Why do I do the things I do?

- Why are there tragedies in my life?
- Why can't I be happy?

- Why can't I make more money?

- Why don't people understand what I'm trying to tell them?

While this approach is important to note—and often effective—it is not for everyone. And although sometimes effective, it often takes years to produce lasting results.

I began to wonder if we have simply been asking the wrong question!

Having studied various techniques of counseling for years, and been witness to the fact that there were many people who would not or could not benefit from traditional therapy, I began to wonder if we have simply been asking the wrong question!

Perhaps I could help my clients more quickly and easily if we focused on the HOW! That's when I decided to adopt a solution-focused approach to helping my clients.

And I'm so glad I did, since my clients are so much happier and getting extraordinary results!

As a solution-focused counselor I help my clients find solutions to their problems as quickly as possible. The process of discovering HOW happens incredibly fast. I teach my clients that the same energy used to analyze the problem can be used to generate solutions!

That's what happens when you work with me! We begin the transformation process by focusing on how to find solutions to create EFFORTLESS CHANGE. And we help you create lasting transformations.

Now, here's the really interesting part: After helping literally thousands of people, no one seems interested in the WHY after their life has been optimized and transformed by the HOW! Awesome, huh?

Ashley Miller's Story

"I knew I was just coasting along on cruise control...And sure, I'd get a burst of wind into my sails and jump ahead for a few days. But it never lasted! I wasn't really depressed or even unhappy; it's just that everything in my life was like a B-minus or a C-plus...

...I saw James do a presentation, and he said a couple of things that really stood out. He asked what we thought our life would look like if we were achieving our maximum and full potential, being

more productive, MORE ALIVE, being the best person we could be.

I had to be honest with myself, and that's when I called James.

My first meeting with James was awesome, and he dug right in, but in such a warm and friendly and caring manner. It was absolutely clear, and I KNEW that James had one purpose: to transform my life…to get me to an A or even an A-plus!

And now I can tell you that I've never been more settled with myself, and I've never been happier in my life…EVER!"

Have you ever wondered what life would look like if you got "un-stuck?"

How would it feel to have complete clarity, to have complete work/life balance, to have the best relationships ever, knowing that you're running at optimum levels in every aspect of your life, achieving extraordinary results?

Just imagine…you'd be making the best possible decisions; you'd be infinitely more creative, more productive, more successful; you'd be healthier, wealthier and HAPPIER THAN EVER!

Tom is right! As many of my clients often say, "If I'd have known how easy it was to get a life coach, I would have started sooner!" I tell them that I'm just happy that they are doing it now! I'm happy you're pursuing your goals!

In our coaching program, Mary, Tom, Stephanie, Ashley and thousands of others received the tools, strategies and support they needed to achieve extraordinary results.

I helped them change their MINDSET by renewing their unlimited beliefs. I helped them transformed their lives and their businesses. I provided them the tips, strategies and support needed to achieve their goals.

My clients and I have used the following 5 Steps to renew our minds and to achieve EXTRAORDINARY results. You're encouraged to implement these steps to change your MINDSET and change your life!

5 Steps to Change Your MINDSET

"The mind is just like a muscle: the more you exercise it, the stronger it gets, and the more it can expand."
Idowu Koyenikan

I believe that if you change your MINDSET and take positive actions toward your goals, you will change your life. You cannot change the reality of life, but you can change your thinking and your life.

You can change any MINDSET if you want to. However, the need to change must be a recognized priority. God has given you the power to change your life by giving you the tools to think, feel and accomplish your goals.

If you change your MINDSET, you'll change your life! If you believe in your dreams and take action toward your destiny, you will change your life! Here are 5 steps to change your MINDSET:

1. Recognize and acknowledge the current MINDSET preventing your success

Is limiting belief holding you back from achieving your goals? The first step to changing your MINDSET is to identify and acknowledge your limiting beliefs. We all have some limiting beliefs and negative thoughts that adversely impact our lives.

The quicker you identify your limiting beliefs, the faster you can take action to overcome them. Take inventory of what goes in your mind. Pay close attention to your thought pattern; and ensure that it's consistent with your current goals. If you want positive results in your life, practice positive thinking and take actions toward your goals.

One of the best ways to change your thinking is to replace your limiting belief. What's a BELIEF? It's a state of mind or habit in which trust is placed in some person or something. Synonyms for belief include faith, trust, confidence and persuasion.

Limiting beliefs can stop us from achieving our full potential.

Our beliefs create the maps that guide our goals and empower us to take action. The challenge is that eighty percent (80%) of our beliefs are based on our past experiences between ages of three and seven (3-7). Also, the interpretations of painful events and some pleasurable experiences play a major role in shaping our belief system.

Our beliefs determine how we think, feel and behave. Limiting beliefs can stop us from achieving our full potential. They can cause to take no action toward our goals. They can even cause us to miss out on opportunities that will transform our lives.

What is a goal that you have always wanted to achieve and haven't? Why haven't you? Whatever the reason, there's always a limiting belief preventing your success.

Limiting Beliefs Preventing Your Success

"The only thing that's keeping you from getting what you want is the story you keep telling yourself."
Tony Robins

We all have unlimited potential. However, our results often don't reflect that. Why? It's simply because our unconscious beliefs hinder our results.

What limiting belief is preventing *your* success? The quicker you identify your limiting beliefs, the faster you can implement a plan to overcome them. I recently read an eBook by Tony Robins that helps in identifying some of these factors.

4 Basic Limiting Beliefs Preventing Success

1. **HEALTH**: "I don't have time for health and fitness."

FACT: Twenty-six percent of people think they do not have enough time to make a lifestyle change for their health. The truth is, we all have the same number of hours in a day. Why are some people able to capture every moment while others consistently use lack of time as an excuse? They make health a priority. It's a **MUST** for them, and for others it's a SHOULD.

To enjoy everyday life, you need your health. Make it a priority and follow your doctor's recommendations.

2. **RELATIONSHIPS**: "I don't deserve love."

FACT: Insecurity is fatal to your relationship. In fact, it's one of the top 10 reasons marriages end in divorce. To overcome insecurity, you must decide to believe that you deserve love, maximize your strength while improving your limitations. In order to find and keep love, you must first overcome the false belief that you are unworthy of love.

3. **SUCCESS**: "Successful people are just lucky."

FACT: If there is one thing successful people have in common, it is *not* luck. Instead, they all share key personality traits such as clear goals, purpose, passion, persistence, drive and commitment.

My wife and I started more than 10 businesses before one succeeded. We succeeded because we remained committed to our goals. Here's a formula we used as a guide for success:

Beliefs + Capability + Action = Successful Results

4. **MONEY**: "I am just not good with money."

FACT: Over 60% of Americans report not having a spending, saving and investment plan. It's hard to be good at anything if you do not have an effective strategy for success. To achieve your financial goals, enlist the help of processional advisors and take actions.

Five Common Places where our Beliefs Come From

- Our environment
- The events of our life
- Our knowledge base
- Our results in life
- Our vision of the future

Once you've identified the limiting belief preventing your success, the next step is to decide to replace it.

2. The Decision

Make the decision that you want to change your limiting beliefs. Learn to hear your limiting thinking. Talk back to your negative self-talk with a positive voice and attitude.

Ten Powerful Beliefs to Create an Extraordinary Life

1. I deserve to be loved. Love is always available when my heart is opened.

2. Everything is going to be all right. I accept 100 percent responsibility for my actions and results.

3. I'm learning something new every day. Every experience is an opportunity to grow and to enjoy the gift of life. Everyone I meet is a friend, a client or a business partner to be developed.

4. I choose to give my best in life and at work.

5. Everything I want or need, I must earn it. No one owes me anything.

6. I choose to give before receiving.

7. I'm free to be ME!

8. With the help of my team, I can do all things!

9. I'm abundantly blessed to be a blessing to others.

Daily positive affirmations, meditation and prayer have proved effective in reframing our limiting thinking. In the Notes section of this book, I provide a list of positive affirmations to get you started.

3. New perspective
Get a new perspective by getting new information to replace your limiting thinking. Read a new book and find new ways to get new information needed to overcome obstacles holding you back. In step 1, I provided you 10 powerful beliefs you can adopt **right now** to create an extraordinary life.

Also, I recommend that you enlist the help of your team members. The team can include professionals such as a life coach or a counselor who can help you change your MINDSET and change your life.

Your team can help you identify your limiting beliefs, recognize that you have a choice, and help you overcome the obstacles preventing your success, joy and happiness.

The team can help you realize that you have the power over your mind. You can **choose** to act according to your positive MINDSET instead of the negative one. More importantly, your team can help you develop a new plan to reframe your thinking and condition new behaviors that lead to lasting success.

4. Self-Care

One of the best ways to change your psychology is to change your physiology. When you take good care of your body, it positively affects your mind, your spirit and your entire life. Physical health helps you gain clarity, vitality and strength to pursue your goals and enjoy your results.

For physical wellness, start small by taking these steps:

- Get an annual physical and follow your doctor's recommendations

- Sleep 8 hours per day

- Eat regularly and intake lots of fruits and vegetables in your diet. Consult your nutritionist and doctor.

- Exercise for 30 minutes 3 times per week. This can include walking, swimming and biking. Before starting any exercise, I recommend that you consult your doctor.

5. Success Planning

Everything you need for your breakthrough is within your reach. However, you must **plan** for your success.

Changing your MINDSET is a process, and to succeed, a plan is essential. As quoted by Benjamin Franklin, "If you fail to plan, you plan to fail."

Success leaves clues. Successful people always plan. Follow their footsteps and plan for your success. Take positive actions to change your thinking and your life.

Remember, you are not alone in the journey of life. I'm here to help you! I wrote this book to give you the essential tools, strategies and support you need to achieve extraordinary results!

Help is available, but you must ask for it and seek it. For coaching, feel free to email me by visiting CoachJamesJustin.com!

"To change your life, you have to change yourself. To change yourself, you have to change your MINDSET."
Wilson Kanadi

The Mindset Change Cycle

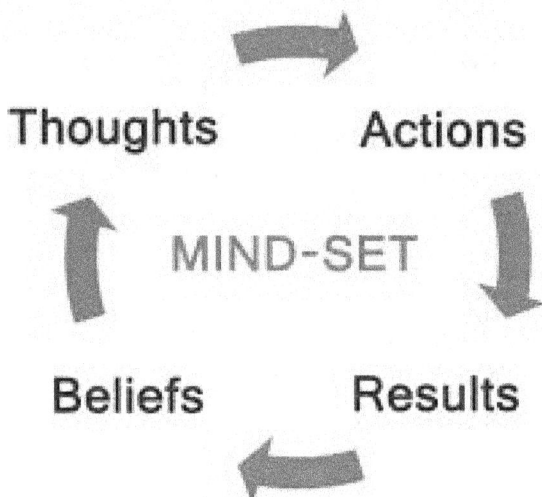

Thoughts   Actions

MIND-SET

Beliefs   Results

The mindset change cycle illustrates the flow of changing your mindset and change your life. The process of changing your mindset begins by deciding to control what goes into your mind and take the necessary steps to replace the beliefs preventing your success.

"To transform your life, your desire to change must be greater than your desire to stay the same."
James Justin

Bonus TIPS to Change Your MINDSET and Change Your Life!

• Here's a quick exercise you can use to change your state or when you're feeling nervous about trying something new: Rub your hands together as fast as you can, and then clap them as hard as you can. Repeat this at least three times and you will instantly feel better! Don't believe me? Give it your best try!

• Commit to and develop the environment that fosters high standards for continued education, growth and development. Remember, readers are leaders. And the more you learn, the more you can earn! Keep on practicing the lessons you've discovered in life!

• The best place to start transforming your life is to renew your mind by adopting the growth MINDSET. I know that it's not easy to change your MINDSET, but I encourage you to stay focused on practicing the tips provided in this book. The rewards will be worth it!

• Changing your thinking and your life is a process. It takes willingness and effort. Your desire to change must be greater than your desire to stay the same. Be patient, and remain focused on your goals!

For additional support, tools and strategies to transform your life, visit CoachJamesJustin.com and sign up for our coaching program!

Chapter 4

Change Your EMOTIONS, Change Your Life

"Human behavior flows mainly from their emotions."
Plato

E motions are essential for the human experience. Without our feelings, we would be like robots. We enjoy everyday life through our emotions.

Emotions are a natural, instinctive state of mind. They're driven by the conscious mind, and derived from circumstances, mood and interactions with others.

Your feelings play a vital role in your transformational process. They determine your actions and your results in life and in business.

Your feelings are the gateway to your subconscious mind; and are your true expressions of your heart. As King Solomon declared, "For as he thinks in his heart, so is he."

The 4 Basic Human Emotions

As human beings, we experience all kinds of emotions every day. Sometime, we may even feel that we are experiencing all the emotions in the wheel. Paul Ekman, the American psychologist who pioneered the relationship between emotion and facial expression, suggested that there are six basic human emotions: anger, happiness, surprise, disgust, sadness and fear.

Before he published his findings in the early 1970s, it was widely believed that facial expressions and their meanings were specific to every culture. For more information on Ekman's psychological view of human emotions, read the book, "Emotion in the Human Face."

New research on human emotions suggests that there are only four basic emotional groups. All other emotions can be grouped into one of these emotions:

1. **Joy / Happiness**
2. **Sadness / Depress**
3. **Fear / Anxiety**
4. **Anger / Disgust**

This research was conducted by the Institute of Neuroscience and Psychology at the University of Glasgow. The research finding was published in the Current Biology Journal.

The Disney Pixar hit movie "Inside Out" gives a great visual of our emotional state. I highly recommend that you watch it to gain a deeper understanding of your emotions.

List of Popular Emotions

Use the list below to identify what you're feeling now.

ANGER	FEAR	JOY	SAD
Disgust	Anxiety	Happy	Depressed
Mad	Worry	Glad	Disappointed
Fury	Paralyze	Content	Regretful
Rage	Despair	Confident	Dismayed
Irritated	Doubt	Relax	Pessimistic
Annoy	Confuse	Excited	Blue
Impatient	Terror	Relieved	Lonely
Passion	Panic	Thankful	Hurt

I believe that the more you understand your emotions, the more you can manage them and use them to transform your life. Get to know yourself by getting to know your thoughts and emotional patterns, and take one action per day toward your goals!

If you don't manage your emotions, they WILL manage YOU!

As noted by Joel Osteen, *"Every day we have plenty of opportunities to get angry, stressed or offended. But what you're doing when you indulge these negative emotions is giving something outside yourself, power over your happiness. You can choose to not let little things upset you."* Don't sweat the small stuff that life throws at you. Discover how to manage your emotional triggers and take positive actions toward your goals.

Emotional Triggers

Our brain is powerful! One of the functions of your brain is its ability to rationalize your behavior. An event occurs, you react, and then your brain instantly creates a reason for your reaction that seems to justify your behavior, even if the reason makes no sense. When you discover how to manage your emotional triggers, you'll be able to enjoy your emotions!

What is an Emotional Trigger?

An emotional trigger is a response to a person's thought, dialogue, situations and events that provoke a strong emotional reaction. Your emotions can be triggered by both internal and external stimuli. Your emotional triggers are felt through your senses.

Why is Emotional Mastery important?

Emotional mastery is important because your emotions determine your actions and results. Eighty percent of your decisions are driven by your emotions. Therefore, if you want to transform your life, it's critical to manage your emotions effectively.

When you discover how to manage your emotions, you can use them more efficiently to achieve your desired goals and to enjoy everyday life.

How to Manage Your Emotional Triggers

1. Take 100% responsibility for your emotional reactions.

Acknowledge and accept that you're an emotional being. Your emotions are an important part of being human. They allow you to experience pleasure and pain.

2. Recognize when you're having an emotional reaction as soon as it begins to appear in your body.

In his book, "Looking for Spinoza: Joy, Sorrow and the Feeling Brain," Antonio Damasio noted that at any moment, your rate of breathing, blood flow, muscle tension and constriction in your gut signals a pattern you can identify as a feeling. He also emphasizes the importance of accepting our emotions.

Your emotions are impacting your relationships, job performance, happiness and all areas of your life.

"The sooner you recognize that you are an emotional being, the quicker you can manage your triggers and develop emotional freedom."
Marcia Reynolds

3. Take inventory of your current emotional triggers.

One of the best ways to manage your emotional reactions is to identify your common triggers. For example, one of my triggers is injustice against kids who cannot defend themselves. I often get angry and over reactive when I observe any child being mistreated and neglected.

4. Decide to challenge your emotional triggers.

You have the power to face your emotional triggers. You can choose which emotions you want to feel and which emotional state you live in. Your emotions are driven primarily by your MINDSET. If you redirect your focus, you'll change your emotions. God has given you the power to THINK. If you rephrase your limiting thinking with positive ones, you'll overcome your emotional reactions and transform your life!

When you shift your thinking, you shift your emotions and your life. For example, if you're feeling depressed, go for a walk. As you place your body in motion, your mood will also change. With practice, the reaction to your emotional triggers will subside! When you define your goals, shift into the emotion that will help you get the best results. Here are some actions you can take right now:

> **Meditate**: Choose to focus on one key word that represents how you want to feel, and allow yourself to feel the shift.

> **Pray**: Ask God to guide your life and give you wisdom to achieve your goals.

> **Relax**: Breathe and release the tension in your body.

> **Detach**: Clear your mind of all unwanted thoughts.

5. Commit to self-awareness, mindfulness and continued growth.

The process of personal discovery and development will help you regulate your emotions and take control of your life. Self-awareness is the process of understanding your thoughts, feelings, actions, strengths, weaknesses and interpersonal connections with oneself and others. It is an honest assessment of who you believe you are.

When you're self-aware, you're able to bounce back quicker from emotional triggers, as well as from sifting through unwanted emotional response.

These steps are designed to help you overcome unwanted emotional triggers. As you continue to practice these steps, you'll be able to manage your emotional reactions and develop positive emotional health.

Your emotions are part of the human experience. I urge you to embrace them. They allow you to enjoy an extraordinary life. Instead of controlling your emotions, discover how to manage your reactions to them.

70 Words and Phrases that Trigger *Positive* Thoughts and Emotions

1. I'm positive!
2. I'm happy!
3. I have the power to transform my life!
4. I'm the captain of my life because God gave me the power to think big.
5. I'm bold.
6. I have a definite mission, vision and purpose for my life.
7. I have complete clarity.
8. I have complete focus.
9. I have clear goals and objectives for my life.
10. I achieved my dreams.
11. I can breathe again.
12. I have a new life.
13. I can see a bright and shining future.
14. Unstuck
15. Abundance
16. Everyone and everything I need to create abundance in my life comes with effortless ease.
17. I'm attractive!
18. I'm wealthy!
19. I'm healthy!
20. I have assistance and resources to achieve my dreams.
21. I experience many breakthroughs.
22. I have all the transferable skills required for my success.
23. I have no limits.
24. Alive
25. I can breathe again.
26. I'm a contributing member of my society.
27. My responsibilities are manageable.
28. I can play and enjoy life again.
29. I'm confident, with high self-worth and self-esteem.
30. I am fearfully and wonderfully made.
31. I'm deeply loved.
32. I'm blessed.
33. God loves me!
34. Excited

35. Restful
36. Peaceful
37. Choices
38. My possibilities are endless.
39. I can do all things.
40. I have the power to manage and overcome fear.
41. I'm relaxed and stress-free.
42. I can see the light at the end of the tunnel!
43. Unstoppable
44. I'm living life on my terms.
45. I'm generous!
46. I'm free!
47. Wanted
48. Winner
49. Grateful
50. Forgiveness
51. Daily hope
52. Full potential achieved.
53. Joyful
54. Brilliant
55. Superb
56. Radiant
57. Thoughtful
58. Insightful
59. Energetic
60. Inspired
61. Empowered
62. Helpful
63. Decisive
64. Resplendent
65. Driven
66. Successful
67. Autonomy
68. Discipline
69. I have the power to transform, to optimize and to accelerate my life success!
70. I'm living life to the fullest!

70 Words and Phrases that Trigger *Negative* Thoughts and Emotions

1. Negative
2. I feel dead inside.
3. I'm depressed.
4. Hopeless
5. Lost
6. Despondent
7. Grief
8. My life is over...finished.
9. I'm stuck.
10. Trapped
11. Afraid
12. Devastated
13. Nobody wants me.
14. There's a giant stop sign on my life.
15. No progress
16. No dream
17. No future
18. I'm not college material.
19. Worthless
20. Poor me.
21. Useless
22. Can't breathe
23. Choked
24. Strangled
25. I'm going nowhere.
26. Bad relationships.
27. Low energy.
28. Trauma
29. My past is holding me back.
30. I'm a victim.
31. it's not my fault.
32. I'm a failure.
33. I have no power.
34. Use / Abuse

35. Bad habits
36. I don't contribute to society.
37. I'm a lost case.
38. I'm not a good parent.
39. I'm not a role model for my children.
40. I'm stupid.
41. Scared
42. Frozen
43. The world hates me.
44. Life sucks.
45. I feel like I'm in a dark tunnel.
46. I can't see the light.
47. I'm a burden.
48. I'm in despair.
49. I'm miserable.
50. Struggle
51. Anger
52. Resentment
53. Bitterness
54. Rejection
55. Betrayal
56. Abandonment
57. Hopeless
58. Disappointment
59. Exhaustion
60. Unloved
61. No boundary.
62. Ungrateful
63. Corroded
64. Loser
65. My life is a sad story.
66. Insecure
67. No one cares about me.
68. I have no friends.
69. I've nothing to give.
70. I am nothing.

Emotional Intelligence

It takes more than a high intelligence quotient (IQ) to transform your life and your business. Your emotional intelligence (EI) is equally important. It has a marked impact on your ability to accept yourself, to build strong relationships, manage occupational stress and minimize personal and professional risks.

So, what is emotional intelligence, and what practical value does it have for success?

Traditionally, we were taught that emotional responses to life events distort objectivity and reasoning. Therefore, it should be suppressed, especially in the workplace.

Most contemporary psychologists believe that emotional intelligence is equally important to success as intelligence quotient. Lack of emotional mastery may have a negative impact on our ability to perform a range of critical, intellectual and social tasks.

Research suggests that individuals can improve their ability to communicate, manage stress, make sound judgments and even utilize a higher degree of their IQ, not by suppressing emotion, but by enhancing their emotional intelligence.

What is Emotional Intelligence?

Emotional Intelligence, or Emotional Quotient (EQ), is the ability to identify and discriminate between an individual's own emotions and those of others, to best guide their thoughts, decisions and actions.

> *"Emotional intelligence is your ability to identify and manage your own emotions and the emotions of others."*
> **Daniel Goleman**

Emotionally intelligent people can perceive their emotions, discern the cause and respond appropriately to achieve a desired outcome. While this may sound simplistic, it can have an extremely powerful impact on your success.

Why is High Emotional Intelligence Beneficial?

A key benefit of cultivating emotional intelligence is self-awareness. Self-awareness is about knowing who you are. It's the foundation of personal growth and development. When you know yourself, you are better prepared to understand others. And the more you understand yourself, the more you can open your heart to God to transform your life.

I agree that getting to know yourself is a process. It's a journey down the Yellow Brick Road to success and happiness. Daniel Goleman, the American psychologist and author of "Emotional Intelligence," calls self-awareness the "keystone" of emotional intelligence.

When you are self-aware, you'll have the power to develop yourself and to develop healthier relationships.

Emotional intelligence also promotes the ability to strategically communicate, by perceiving another person's emotions, and understanding their reaction to certain situations. This allows you to avoid conflicts, promote positive exchanges and instill trust in a relationship. Such skills can dramatically enhance your ability to negotiate, persuade and build loyalty in your personal and professional life.

Similarly, emotional intelligence enlightens your ability to stop the escalation of one's own negative emotions resulting from personal and occupational stressors.

Research has revealed that "unchecked" negative emotional triggers limit an individual's ability to explore thoughts that promote new methods or solutions.

The more you explore your emotions, the more you can manage them effectively.

"Your intellect may be confused sometime, but your emotions will never lie to you."
Roger Ebert

"Feelings or emotions are the universal language and are to be honored. They are the authentic expression of who you are at your deepest place."
Judith Wright

The 3 Greatest Forces that Influence Your Emotional Health

Emotional health leads to success in work, relationships and health. People who are emotionally healthy are in control of their emotions and their behaviors. They express their emotions more effectively. They are better equipped to more effectively handle life's challenges, build strong relationships and recover from setbacks.

Of the many factors in life that influence your emotions, there are three common forces that determine what you feel:

1. Your Psychology
Your thinking determines your feeling; your feeling determines your action, and your action determines your result. If you want a new result in your life, start by changing your MINDSET. Shift your thinking from negative to positive.

2. Your Physiology
This process deals with the functions and activities of daily living. The ability to comfortably and effectively perform your daily activities plays a major role in your emotions. It helps you by developing confidence. Your physical and chemical balance is very important on how you feel. If you feel any discomfort or constant pain in your body, don't ignore it. Make an appointment with your doctor as soon as possible to ensure that your body is functioning normally.

3. Your Story

What's the theme of your life story? Does the story you tell yourself build you up or tear you down? The story you tell yourself will indeed affect your mood. Language is powerful!

The words you speak over yourself will influence your mood. For example, if you consistently saying, "I'll never be happy," unhappiness will become your life's companion and you'll be sad. "The tongue has the power of life and death, and those who love it will eat its fruit" (King Solomon).

If you change the theme of your story from a negative to a positive one, you'll change your life!

Instead of saying "I'll never be happy," ask yourself, "What lesson can I learn from my current situation, and how can I be happy right now?"

You have a powerful story. Find it, own it and use it! Reframe your story from negative to positive. Take action toward your goals, and watch your life transform!

Your emotions are important to your transformation because they influence your actions and your habits.

The habits that you practice consistently will determine your results. If you want to transform your life, you must check your habits and make changes as needed to achieve your goals.

Defense Mechanisms

Defense mechanism is another factor that Influences our emotional health. In order to deal with internal conflicts and problems in life, Sigmund Freud stated that we employ various defense mechanisms to maintain a balanced life...to protect ourselves from feelings of anxiety or guilt, which arise because we feel threatened.

Defense mechanisms such as repression or projection are mental processes initiated unconsciously to avoid conscious conflict or anxiety. Review Chapter 2 for details on how the mind works. The chart below illustrates the common defenses.

6 Common Defense Mechanisms

Mechanism	Description	Example
Repression	Repression is an unconscious mechanism employed by the ego to keep disturbing or threatening thoughts from becoming conscious.	During the Oedipus complex aggressive thoughts about the same sex parents are repressed
Denial	Denial involves blocking external events from awareness. If some situation is just too much to handle, the person just refuses to experience it.	For example, smokers may refuse to admit to themselves that smoking is bad for their health.
Projection	This involves individuals attributing their own unacceptable thoughts, feeling and motives to another person.	You might hate someone, but your superego tells you that such hatred is unacceptable. You can 'solve' the problem by believing that they hate you.
Displacement	Satisfying an impulse (e.g. aggression) with a substitute object.	Someone who is frustrated by his or her boss at work may go home and kick the dog,
Regression	This is a movement back in psychological time when one is faced with stress.	A child may begin to suck their thumb again or wet the bed when they need to spend some time in the hospital.
Sublimation	Satisfying an impulse (e.g. aggression) with a substitute object. In a socially acceptable way.	Sport is an example of putting our emotions (e.g. aggression) into something constructive.

Chapter 5

Change Your HABIT, Change Your Life

"Life transformation is not an act, but a habit."
James Justin

D id you know that 80% of your results in life come from your habits? Developing good habit is an important step to transform your life and achieve your extraordinary results.

A habit is any action you do on a regular basis. According to the American Journal of Psychology (1903), "A habit is a particular way of thinking, willing, or feeling acquired through repetition of a mental experience. It's the process by which new behaviors become automatic."

We all have good and bad habits. However, how we manage our habits will determine our results. Bad habits deter you from your goals, while good habits draw you closer to your goals. Aristotle once noted, *"We are what we repeatedly do."* Therefore, if you want to change your life, you must take inventory of your habits and make the necessary shifts.

How Habit is Formed

Habit is formed through repetition. Generally, we repeat the same thoughts, the same actions and the same experiences until they are conditioned within our being.

According to Psychology Today, habit formation is the process by which new behaviors become automatic. That's because the behavioral patterns we repeat most often are literally etched into our neural pathways. The good news is that, through repetition, it's possible to form—and maintain—new habits.

Good habits bring us closer to our goals, while bad habits draw us away from our achievements.

7 Habits of Highly Effective People

In his book, "The 7 Habits of Highly Effective People," Stephen R. Covey provides us the habits needed to transform our lives. This book is a practical guide to the law of habit. I encourage you to read the book and practice what you discover.

Here is a summary of Covey's 7 habits of highly effective people:

Habit #1: "Be Proactive"

Your transformation begins from within. Become a highly effective person by making decisions to improve your life through the things that influence you, rather than by simply reacting to external forces. Plan, position and promote yourself toward your goals. Success and transformation happen to those who planned for it!

Habit #2: "Begin with the End in Mind"

Develop your Mission, Vision, Purpose (MVP) statement, your core values and goals for your life and your business. In the Notes section of this book, I added a value assessment worksheet you can use to identify your core values. My clients find it helpful in prioritizing their values, and setting goals according to the most important elements in their life. I believe that you will find it useful as well.

Develop a strategic plan to achieve your MVP. You can break down your MVP into short-term and long-term goals, with specific objectives and time frames for completion.

Enlist the help of winners. A life coach, a counselor or a mentor are great professionals to have on your team.

Habit #3: "First Things First" (Prioritize your Life)

Invest your time, money, energy and all other resources wisely. Focus your thinking, feeling and activities on the things that give you the greatest results, happiness and fulfillment.

Prioritize your life around your MVP, core values and your loved ones.

Take time to plan and develop a life/work balance. Enlist the help of your team and your advisors to keep you accountable.

Habit #4: "Think Win-Win"

Seek agreements and relationships that are mutually beneficial.

Resolve conflicts quickly by "letting go" of things beyond your control, and practice the virtue of forgiveness. The Serenity Prayer is a great daily affirmation to meditate on. To discover how prayer works, get a copy of our book "The Power of Prayer" on Amazon or at CoachJamesJustin.com!

When Win/Win deals cannot be achieved, accept the fact that agreeing to make "no deal" may be the best alternative at that moment.

Habit #5: "Seek First to Understand, then to be understood"

Nurture healthy relationships with people by seeking to understand them before requesting that they understand you.

You'll attract whatsoever you project. For example, if you want a new friend, you must first *become* one. If you want to succeed in life and in business, develop close relationship with people who can help you achieve your goals while you're helping *them* as well.

One of the best ways to attract the right people in your life is to become the friend *you* want to attract. Before you require people to understand you, you must first strive to understand them. I recommend that you start practicing this principle with your family and current friends. When you are ready, you can extend this practice with others. Whatsoever you give, you shall receive. In the words of Zig Ziglar, *"If you help enough people get what they want, they'll help you get what you want."*

One of the best ways to practice this habit is to develop your communication skills. Listen more and speak less. You cannot discover anything without first listening.

The habit of listening is a valuable tool in your efforts toward building healthy relationships. For more details, get a copy of our book **"7 Steps to Develop Healthy Relationships with Anyone,"** available on Amazon and at CoachJamesJustin.com.

Habit #6: "Synergize"

Synergize is the habit of creative cooperation. It involves teamwork, an open mind and a desire to thrive in the adventure of finding new solutions to old problems.

Teamwork doesn't just happen on its own. It's a process; and through that process, each team member contributes their unique and personal experience and expertise.

Develop healthy relationship with those who can help you achieve your goals while you are helping them succeed.

This is a great habit to develop if you want to succeed. Success is a team sport.

Find people who share your passion, and partner with them to make the world a better place.

Habit #7: "Sharpen the Saw"

Take time off to recharge, relax and refine your systems to succeed.

Prayer, meditation and sleep are vital tools for relaxation and to renew your spirit, soul and body. They can help you reduce stress, and find balance in life. Do something fun and enjoy everyday life!

To achieve any goal, the right action is required. We are not yet in the level of faith where we can simply imagine our dreams and expect them to become a reality. For example, I cannot stay home watching TV every day and imagine that I'll get my dream job. That's naive thinking. Until I face my fear and take action by truly applying for jobs, I'll never get one.

If you truly want to transform your life, you must develop effective habits that support your success.

To achieve your goals, you must BELIEVE it and TAKE ACTION. As you discover the keys to unlock your miracles and act upon them, your life will be changed for the best.

This book is designed to help you transform your life from ordinary to extraordinary by inspiring you to practice the following success formula:

Positive MINDSET + Positive Habits = Positive Results

Before you can change any habit, it's important to understand the role of your behaviors. Your habits are repetitive behaviors designed to help you avoid pain or attract pleasure.

The habits you developed are conditioned to meet one of the 6 basic human needs. Your habits determine your results in life and in business. That's why I said, if you change your habits, you'll change your life. What habit is preventing your success now?

Why We Do What We Do

"What we do is a direct reflection of our desires. To achieve any goal, we must believe it wholeheartedly and commit to it until it's a reality."
James Justin

There is always a reason why we act a certain way. Our behaviors are not random. One essential factor is our needs. The more you understand your needs, wants, thoughts, feelings and actions, the more you can influence your results in life.

As a child, I was fascinated about why people think, feel and act the way they do. Why some people pursue opportunities that lead to greater success, joy and happiness, while others consistently ignore those same opportunities.

I was curious to know why some people sacrificed their lives for others, while some will murder a family member, a friend or a stranger for their own personal gain. Why people such as Jesus Christ, Mother Teresa, Nelson Mandela and Dr. Martin Luther King, Jr. sacrificed their lives for a cause and the greater good of humanity?

It is my passion to understand the human spirit, psychology and behaviors that led me to earn my master's degree in the field of counseling, and dedicate my life to coaching, speaking and helping people like YOU!

The 6 Basic Human Needs

While each person is unique, we all share similar basic needs. And most of our behaviors are driven by those needs.

According to American psychologist Abraham Maslow, there are six basic human needs that drive our thoughts, feelings and actions.

The Hierarchy of Needs

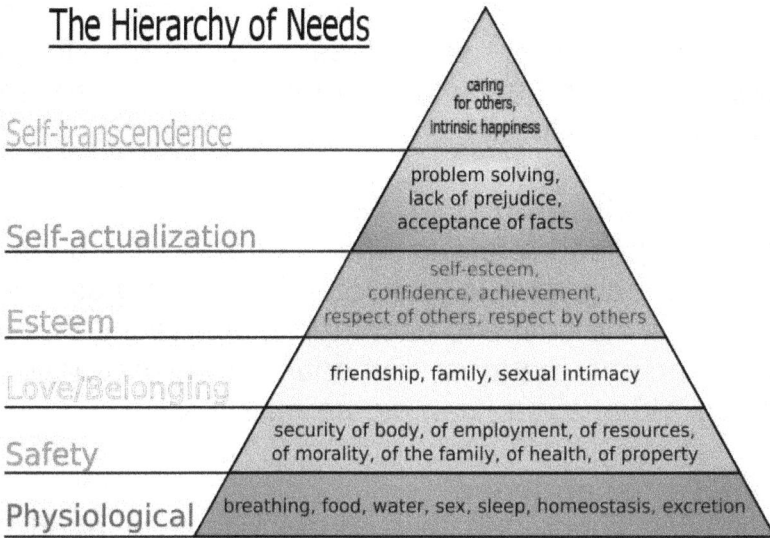

Self-transcendence	caring for others, intrinsic happiness
Self-actualization	problem solving, lack of prejudice, acceptance of facts
Esteem	self-esteem, confidence, achievement, respect of others, respect by others
Love/Belonging	friendship, family, sexual intimacy
Safety	security of body, of employment, of resources, of morality, of the family, of health, of property
Physiological	breathing, food, water, sex, sleep, homeostasis, excretion

1. Physiological Needs
These needs are required for our basic survival, and include air, water, food and sleep.

2. Safety
- Personal security
- Financial security
- Health and well-being

3. Love and Belonging
This need is interpersonal and involves feelings of belonging, connection, love and intimacy.

4. Esteem
All humans have a need to feel respected. This includes the need for self-esteem, self-respect and self-confidence. Esteem encompasses the typical human desire to be socially accepted and valued by others. People often pursue a profession or hobby to gain recognition. These activities give the person a sense of contribution or value.

5. Self-Actualization
This level of need refers to what a person's full potential is, and the realization of that potential. Maslow describes this level as the desire to accomplish everything that one can, to become the most that one can be. According to Maslow, *"What a man can be, he must be."*

6. Self-Transcendence
In his later years, Maslow added the sixth need. He realized that the "self" only finds its actualization in its giving to some higher goal outside oneself, in altruism and spirituality.

These basic needs offer only a psychological view on human behaviors and personality. Review these needs as often as possible to better understand your needs. When you understand your needs and take proactive steps to meet them, it will help you develop new patterns that lead to lasting fulfillment, success, joy and happiness.

How to Overcome Bad Habits

"The only proper way to eliminate bad habits is to replace them with good ones."
Jerome Hines

Bad habits can be reversed. It's not always easy. However, I believe with the deepest desire to change, the right strategy, love and support, you can achieve anything. With God, all things are possible!

Bad habits are learned behaviors repeated over time. Thus, if you change the MINDSET that supports the bad behavior, you'll change your life.

Our habits are created to fill a void. Once you discover the root of the negative habit, you can replace it with a positive one.

My recommendation is to seek professional help to guide you in the process of overcoming a bad habit. The following two models of behavioral changes can also be helpful.

Two Powerful Models of Behavioral Change

"Human behavior is complicated and every person is unique, so the key to change a behavior is to experiment with different tactics and identify what works for YOU."
Juhan Sonin

There are many theories and models about how to make behavioral changes, new or old. In this book, we'll focus on the two most common theories:

1. The Classical and Operant Conditioning Model

2. The Tiny Habits Model

There isn't a one-size-fits-all approach to behavioral change. The key is to work with your professional counselor or coach to find the best method for you.

If at first you don't succeed…try, try and try again. Keep on looking for the best approach that works for you; the approach that matches your learning style, strengths and resources. Let's briefly review the two models to change behaviors!

The Classical and Operant Conditioning Model

Let's start with the established theories of classical and operant conditioning.

Classical Conditioning is a process of changing behavior by rewarding or punishing a subject each time an action is performed. It involves a reflexive behavior by pairing a neutral stimulus with a naturally occurring one. After a certain amount of time, the neutral stimulus alone is sufficient for triggering the reflex. Nobel Prize winner Ivan Pavlov's experimentation with dogs is the most famous example of this type of conditioning.

In his experiments, a sound (neutral stimulus) was made whenever food was given to the dogs. When the dogs saw the food (natural stimulus), they began to salivate (reflex / naturally occurring behavior). Eventually, the dogs would salivate upon hearing the sound alone.

You can apply this theory to yourself by finding positive pairings that enhance behavioral change, or by removing negative associations that reinforce bad habits. For example, if you're in a program to lose weight, and in the past you consumed more calories at night when you got home, then you may want to bring dinner to work for a while, as this will help you manage the triggers that lead to emotional eating.

Operant Conditioning is a type of learning where behavior is controlled by consequences. Key concepts in operant conditioning are positive reinforcement, negative reinforcement, positive punishment and negative punishment. This type of learning uses reinforcement or punishment to shape desired behavior.

If the targeted behavior occurs, a reward is introduced (positive reinforcement) or something undesirable is taken away (negative reinforcement). If the targeted behavior does not occur, a consequence can be introduced in the form of a "positive punishment" (a negative stimulus) or "negative punishment" (the removal of something desirable).

The Tiny Habits Model

This model was developed by Dr. B.J. Fogg, an expert in the psychology of persuasion, and founder of the Persuasive Lab at Stanford University. He developed a fascinating program for behavioral change, which he called "3 Tiny Habits."

Fogg's research on human behavior concluded that only three things change behavior in the long term:

>Option 1.   Have an epiphany

>Option 2.   Change your context (environment)

>Option 3.   Take "baby steps"

To make lasting changes, Dr. Fogg recommends the following steps:

1) Pick specific, rather than abstract goals. For example, instead of a goal like "get into better shape," identify something more specific, such as losing one pound per week, or saving $100 per month for your emergency fund.

2) Start small. If your ultimate goal is to exercise daily, break that into smaller chunks in the beginning, like walking for 30 minutes once a week, and then build on that success.

3) Build the change into your routine. Make the new behavior more natural by building it into your routine of existing habits. For example, you can walk the stairs at your job instead of taking the elevator. The minute walk using the stairs can be used as part of you 30-minute walking goal for the week.

Another way to practice making a potential new habit automatic is to have it done for you! For instance, if you want to contribute $10 per week to your retirement account, ask your employer and bank to establish a direct deposit to that account before you even get paid. For more tips on how to make your personal finance automatic, get a copy of my book "12 Tips to Achieve Financial Freedom: The Simple Guide to Successfully Manage Your Personal Finance!" It's available at CoachJamesJustin.com and on Amazon.

4) Reward yourself. After you've made any change, big or small, reinforce the behavior by giving yourself a reward. The reward can be something simple, like getting a pedicure or getting a full-body massage.

In addition, Dr. Fogg's research reveals that there are three confluence factors needed for change to occur. Confluence means "flowing together." It is used to describe where streams flow together to create a larger stream. The confluence factors are Trigger, Motivation and Ability. Let's briefly explore these terms:

Trigger refers to some type of prompt or reminder to take action. A trigger may be seeing a phrase that you've posted by your desk that reminds you of your goal. An example Dr. Fogg gives as a trigger is when Facebook sends you an email letting you know that you've been tagged in a picture. This email then triggers you to click that link to the picture. That's one of the techniques

Facebook uses to keep you engaged on their social media platform.

Motivation is what causes us to act, whether it is getting a glass of water to reduce thirst or reading a book to gain knowledge. When you believe in a cause, your motivation is strengthened. Dr. Fogg believes in three "core motivators" that impact human behaviors: Sensation, Anticipation and Social Cohesion. **Sensation** refers to the degree of pleasure or pain involved. **Anticipation** relates to feelings of hope and fear. **Social Cohesion** encompasses the level of rejection or acceptance by others.

Ability is the possession of a talent and skill required to perform a current task. Dr. Fogg believes for change to occur, the target behavior must be achievable. For example, if I never exercise, it would be rather impossible for me to beat Usain Bolt in a 200-meter sprint.

To this last point, Dr. Fogg is a big advocate of simplicity and pursuing small changes at a time. Dr. Fogg's model combines methods from both classical and operant conditioning, with the emphasis on starting small and fostering continued, measurable growth.

Chapter 6

How to ACHIEVE Your Extraordinary Life

"Nothing can stop the man and the woman with the right mental attitude from achieving their goals; nothing on earth can help the one with the wrong mental attitude."
Thomas Jefferson

Imagine a world where you're no longer ruled by limited thinking... A world where you're in control of your life, achieving your full potential, claiming 100 percent responsibility for your success, joy and happiness... A world where your dreams come true, where there is no lack, and where you refuse to fall victim to the criticism of others and the hardship of life.

What a world that would be!

A world where you're freed from fears, insecurities and self-doubts...A world where you're empowered to overcome any obstacles preventing your goals...A world where you're making a difference and helping others achieve their goals.

This kind of reality is well within your reach. And you have the power to transform your life and achieve the life of your dreams! This life starts with you, and it starts in your mind. Once you've identified the life you want, it's time to set smart goals to achieve your ideal lifestyle.

This chapter offers you practical steps to set **SMART** goals. My clients and I use these steps to achieve extraordinary results. As you continue to apply the principles taught in this book, you'll be well in your way to achieving to life of your dreams!

Before I share the steps to create an extraordinary life, I want to urge you to identify what you want in life. Research reveals that people with specific goals are more likely to achieve them.

What do you want most in life? In the words of Henry J. Kaiser, *"Having an aim is the key to achieving your best."* To help you get started, I've listed **the seven most common things people want in life**. Which of these goals will you pursue first?

1. People want to be happier.

2. People want to be wealthier. They want to be reasonably prosperous.

3. People want to be healthier.

4. People want to feel safe and secure.

5. People want to have peace of mind, fulfillment, a sense of purpose and passion.

6. People want healthier relationships with their family, friends and others.

7. People want to have hope that the future will be brighter than today.

Are you ready to transform your life?

If so, let's get started!

5 Steps to Achieve an Extraordinary Life

1. Decide what you want, then go for it!

Let's face it, it's impossible to create the life of your dreams if you don't know what it is. Before you do anything else, take some time to map out what the extraordinary life looks like for you. It's important to write down what you want for your life…things such as spiritual health, psychological health, physical health, relational health and financial health. Think about the work you do and the impact you make.

People who define what they want in life and in business are far more likely to achieve them.

To complete this task, take one minute per day to pray, to meditate and to visualize the life of your dreams. Write down the Mission, the Vision and the Purpose (MVP) for your life and for your business. Once you've identified your MVP, set smaller goals to achieve it.

Once you've identified the life of your dreams, it's time to break down those dreams into smaller, achievable goals.

2. Develop a strategy to achieve your goals.

A strategy is a plan of action or policy designed to achieve a specific goal and objective. Write down your specific goals and objectives to achieve the life of your dreams. As needed, adjust your strategy as you go, then select the one that gives you the greatest results and fulfillment.

A strategy is a specific plan to achieve a desired result or an outcome that you envision, plan and commit to achieve. For example, you may decide that you want to focus on your physical health.

If your goal is to lose 10 pounds this year, to achieve that goal you'll do the following:

•Complete an annual physical with your family doctor.

•Eat three healthy meals as prescribed by your doctor.

•Walk for 30 minutes, three times every day.

3. Develop a winning team

Success is a team sport; don't pursue it alone. As a team, you can achieve success more quickly and easily. Develop a list of professionals who can help you achieve the life and the business of your dreams. Enlist the help of your team, and allow the members of your team to help you while you help them as well.

Your winning team may include a professional coach, counselor, lawyer, accountant, physician, pastor and trusted friends.

"Talent wins games, but teamwork and intelligence win championships."

Michael Jordan

4. Take Action.

One of the biggest obstacles preventing your success is fear. However, to transform your life or your business, you must take some action despite your fear. Your professional team can help you overcome your fear and hold you accountable to achieve your goals. If you take one step every day toward your goal, you will soon achieve the life of your dreams.

Take a calculated risk to achieve the life of your dreams! Taking effective actions will bring you closer toward your goal. Here are some actions you can take every day toward your transformation and success:

• Create a daily routine for your transformation

• Pray for yourself, your goals and for others.

• Consistently feed your mind positive affirmation on what you want.

• Celebrate every progress, big and small.

• Develop an attitude of gratitude.

• Ask for help.

• Introduce yourself to a leader and a new friend.
• Offer your services and products.

• Learn a new skill.

• Read biographies of successful people.

• Hire a professional counselor or life coach.

• Join a group.

• Kiss your spouse.

• Tell your kids you love them.

• Call an old friend and reconnect

• JUST DO ONE THING—EVERY DAY—TO
  TRANSFORM YOUR LIFE!

It's easy to live with excuses and justifications about why you can't do what you want. But inaction, above all, will adversely impact your success. The good news is that nothing is more powerful in defeating fear than action.

"One of the greatest discoveries a man makes, one of his great surprises, is to find he can do what he was afraid he couldn't do"
Henry Ford

5. Reframe your problems into solutions

Every problem contains an opportunity for discovery. If you recognize the lessons from your setbacks, you can use them as fuel for your comebacks. Enlist the help of your team to help you find the silver lining in your cloud. You also can implement this tip by developing patience and a flexible attitude toward life's uncertainties.

Develop patience and a flexible attitude toward life's uncertainties.

If you are facing any difficulties or problems, remember that you are not alone. And I encourage you to face your challenges with your team, and seek God's help in prayer and meditation on his promises. *"These things I have spoken to you, that in Me you may have peace. In the world, you will have tribulation; but be of good cheer, I have overcome the world" (John 10:10).* I pray for you that God's everlasting love gives you peace. *"What then shall we say to these things? If God is for us, who can be against us?" (Romans 8:31).*

Remember, it's not your problems that keep you from creating the life of your dreams; it's the story you tell yourself about them. You're bigger and stronger than your mountains. Don't let them stop you from achieving your goals.

"See things as they are, but not worse than they are. Your problems are really just invitations to step through fear."
Tony Robins

"Crystallize your goals. Make a plan for achieving them and set yourself a deadline. Then, with supreme confidence, determination and disregard for obstacles and other people's criticisms carry out your plan."
Paul J. Meyer

"The difference between average people and achieving people is their perception of and response to failure."
John C. Maxwell

"Review your goals twice every day in order to be focused on achieving them."
Les Brown

BONUS TIPS TO ACHIEVE AN EXTRAORDINARY LIFE

1. Commit to continuous self-improvement.

Life is the greatest teacher. It will continue to teach you lessons needed for continued growth. Therefore, I encourage you to become a student for life and keep on discovering something new every day! *"Live as if you were to die tomorrow. Learn as if you were to live forever"* (Gandhi).

2. Live life with passion.

If you don't develop your own values, people and organizations will tell you how to live your life. That's why I encourage you to prioritize your life and live it to the fullest based on your core values. For details on this principle, visit my blog page at CoachJamesJustin.com. I also included my value assessment worksheet in the Notes section of this book to help you prioritize your life according to your values. Complete this worksheet and let me know your progress by visiting CoachJamesJustin.com.

3. Live to Give.

Developing an attitude of giving back is essential to happiness, joy and success. When you give back to others, you prepare yourself to receive more blessings. The more you help others succeed, the more YOU succeed. When you give back in any way or form, do it willingly, from love and wisdom.

7 Steps for Effective Goal Setting

In an effort to gain a greater perspective into personal development, I listen to at least one audio book per month. One of my favorite topics is goal setting, and one of my favorite programs on that topic is "See You at the Top," by Zig Ziglar. He offered seven powerful steps to effective goal setting, which I will share with you. I also include my own personal examples.

Take the time and write down your responses to all of the seven steps when you're to set your own goals. Writing your goals down makes the goals real; it makes them tangible.

By writing your goals down permanently onto a sheet of paper, it keeps you from mentally bailing on these very important parts of your life. In fact, before you read the seven steps, get a piece of paper or a journal, as well as something to write with.

Setting a goal and doing it right can take a lot of time. Zig Ziglar suggests putting over 20 hours into the more complex goals. He also says that this time will expand to 3-10 hours a week for the rest of your life, once you learn how to set goals effectively.

This is a great payoff for us forward thinkers. If you set aside enough time to do this right, you will be rewarded.

What is goal setting?

Goal setting is the development of an action plan designed to motivate and guide a person or group toward a specific goal. It's a major component of personal and professional development.

Seven Benefits of Goal Setting

In 1979, the Harvard MBA program conducted a study where graduate students were asked, "have you set clear, written goals for your future and made plans to accomplish them?" Only 3% had written goals and plans. 13% had goals but they weren't in writing, and 84% had no goals at all. 10 years later, the same group was interviewed again. The 13% of the class who had goals but did not write them down was earning twice the amount of the 84% who had no goals. The 3% who had written goals were earning, on average, ten times as much as the other 97% of the class combined!

To achieve lasting success, you need to first commit to making a change. Setting SMART goals is the first step in turning your dreams into reality. Right now, take a moment to map out your goals. Make sure the results you are moving toward are specific, measurable, achievable, realistic and timely.

There are many benefits for writing and pursuing your goals. Eighty percent of people who set "SMART" goals actually achieve them. It was Benjamin Franklin who wrote, *"If you fail to plan, you plan to fail."* Here are seven reasons why you set smart goals:

1. Writing a specific goal gives you clearer focus.

2. It optimizes your resources.

3. It helps to manage your time and activities more effectively.

4. It gives you greater peace of mind.

5. It helps to clarify your decision-making process.

6. It makes it easier to communicate with others.

7. It makes it easier to measure your progress.

7 Steps to Set SMART Goals

Specific
Measurable
Attainable
Realistic
Time-sensitive

Step 1: State the Goal

When people ask you about your goals, ambitions and what you want to do with your life, how do you answer? Perhaps you use terms such as "sorta" or "kinda," as in, "I sorta want to go back to school, but I'm not sure." If your answer takes more than a minute to explain, you probably aren't exactly sure what you want to do! Your lack of clarity to questions such as this will make it tough for you to achieve what it is you "sorta kinda" want.

Clearly state your goal in a positive and succinct way. Even if you aren't 100% sure at that moment whether or not you can even achieve the goal, do not insert any "maybes" or "probablys" In your thoughts or statements on this.

If you think losing 30 pounds would be good for you, and that you might want to make it a goal, boldly proclaim:

"I'm losing 30 pounds by December 31."

Author Brian Tracy also suggests that you phrase your goals in present terms, as if you've already completed it. "I have lost 30 pounds by July 31, 2020."

I currently write down my three major goals every single day when I wake up, and I review them before I go to bed. This is another nugget of Brian Tracy's wisdom. But to start implementing this technique, write down your goals in this way once, and see how it makes you feel. Getting things out of your head and onto paper is a great first start.

Step 2: Set a Deadline

Add a deadline to your goal to enhance the clarity even further. This can be a particular date, a month, a year, or even a lifetime goal. If you don't have a deadline to complete the goal, it will never happen. Life often gets in the way. Having a deadline also helps with procrastination.

It will be easier if you start with a few goals that you expect to attempt in the near future.

"I want to increase my monthly income 20% by June, 2020." Or, to be more specific…

"I want to increase my monthly income from $3,000 a month to $3,600 a month by June 2020."

Step 3: Identify the Obstacles

Ask your team members to help you identify obstacles that can prevent you from achieving your goals. By recognizing the things that are in the way of a goal, you can figure out ways to overcome them. Motivational speaker Jim Rohn uses a wonderful football analogy to explain obstacles.

Picture yourself on the field of an empty football stadium. You tuck the ball under your arm and cross the goal line. Should you feel good about yourself? Did you just score a touchdown? No, of course not. There was no resistance, no opposing team. All you did was walk with a ball on a field.

Now, picture yourself on that same field, but now you're in a real game, in a stadium packed with fans. If you cross the goal line with the ball in this situation, you will have scored a touchdown, and you will be cheered and congratulated by your team and fans. You actually accomplished something. You achieved a goal despite the obstacles against you. You did something that was worth it.

Don't just go for the easy stuff. Push forward and take on goals with a few obstacles.

Step 4: Develop a Winning Team that can Help You Achieve the Goal

Success is a team sport. Don't pursue it alone. Identify the people, groups and organizations that can assist you in your quest. You may have to do some research in assembling your Success Team, but your goal is worth the amount of time you invest in it.

For a weight goal, ask your doctor to help you. For improving your income, there are local finance groups and seminars led by speakers who have achieved a great deal of success, and are also willing to help others achieve their own success. You don't have to look far for a coach or counselor. As your coach, I'm here to help you! Contact me by visiting CoachJamesJustin.com!

Step 5: List the Benefits of Achieving the Goal

This is the fun part, where we can let the imagination run wild. List as many benefits as you can think of and ask your team to help you achieve them.

If you want to lose 30 pounds, think about and visualize how much more you will be able to do without hauling that extra weight around. Maybe you will be able to bike more or meet new people in more athletic settings and activities.

If it's a money goal, your achievement award may be to finally afford eating at that new restaurant in town, or take a nice vacation. Whatever your goal is, don't skimp on writing down all the possible spoils of making this goal a reality.

Step 6: List the Skills You Need to Attain the Goal

This is a crucial step in achieving your goal. If you don't have the skills needed to achieve a goal, pay someone to help you. This can help you save time and money.

Perhaps you need to learn web design or a sales technique to increase your monthly income. Or maybe you must learn how to iron your clothes better to look good for that upcoming job interview. There are many books available on so many topics, and there is a growing "how to" directory of videos and articles on the internet, offering an array of skills you can learn. If you need a skill in order to improve your chances of accomplishing a goal, you have no excuse. Take the time and learn it, or hire an expert to help you.

Step 7: Develop a Plan

You have identified your goals, how they will benefit you, and a deadline to achieve them. You have identified your obstacles and assembled a team to help you.

Now, it's the matter of "how."

I suggest compiling a detailed plan for your upcoming week, and how you are going to integrate these six other steps into your daily routine. **When** will you invest the 30 minutes in the library or online, researching the right book for a skill? **When** will you schedule a meeting with that potential mentor about his or her expertise? Also, schedule a twenty-minute period of uninterrupted "down" time for you to meditate and visualize some of the benefits you may receive. If you don't schedule it, you may never move forward.

If you slip up a few times and don't get some actions completed when you planned them, just change the deadline and keep going. The best plans are often adjustable before the end result is reached. Ask your team to keep you accountable to achieve the goal.

This year holds *your* opportunity to achieve some of the goals in your life that you have put off to the side or even forgotten about. Take a few minutes to review and write down your responses to these seven steps right now.

You can use it with any or all of your goals for all areas of your life. Put your answers in a convenient place for you to review often. Pick them up when you have a chance and start working. At that point, the achievement of your goals is simply a matter of time.

I would like to hear from you about your progress. Please email me your success story by visiting CoachJamesJustin.com!

Chapter 7

How to MAINTAIN Your Extraordinary Life

Success leaves clues. You don't need to reinvent the wheel. Find out what successful people do in the areas of your interest, follow their patterns and you will soon have your own success.

James Justin

Are you wondering how you can maintain your success? Well, you're in the right place! This chapter offers you five practical steps to maintain your success.

Successful people will often tell you that luck and hard work got them where they are. But under the surface, there's much more going on. People who rise to top of their fields and maintain their success have much in common.

Ultimately, successful people think and act differently from those who are not so successful. They develop a growth MINDSET to attract and maintain their success.

Learning what sets them apart can help you obtain and maintain your extraordinary life. Jeff Brown, a Harvard Medical School faculty psychologist and co-author of "The Winner's Brain" (DaCapo, 2010), studied highly successful people, looking at their brain activity and life stories for clues to what makes them unique.

He discovered that they think differently than those whose success is short-lived or never comes to pass. According to Brown, "People who are successful have learned to optimize their brains."

He also uncovered strategies he calls "brain power tools," that successful people use to achieve their goals. Each tool is a way of thinking that affects their choices and actions as they work toward a goal. Used as a set, the brain power tools work to help find opportunities, build mastery, work through failures and surpass the status quo.

5 Steps to Lasting Success

Use these tactics in your efforts to consistently reach your goals.

1. Create your own serendipity.
The road to greatness for highly successful people was full of twists and turns. "Successful people take very circuitous paths," Brown says. "They have a real knack for recognizing non-traditional opportunities."

Rather than waiting in a long line of succession, look for paths that others haven't tried. Take on projects that add a unique skill to your toolkit. Find ways to meet people you admire, or pitch yourself for opportunities that seem like an unexpected match. Don't be afraid to get creative. There are many ways to reach every destination.
2. Know what you bring to the table.

Successful people take consistent inventory of their skills and abilities, and they use that mental "feedback" to improve. *"If successful people have a deficit,"* says Brown, *"they want to know it."*

Ask mentors and coaches to help you assess your strengths and weaknesses. Measure your skills as objectively as you can. Then use that information to identify what to learn or practice so that you master strengths and bolster weak skills. And don't shy away from criticism, out of fear or pride. According to Brown, "That's the kiss of death when it comes to success."

3. Focus on a single end goal.
The ability to choose a goal and work toward it without getting distracted is a trademark of highly successful people. "They have laser focus, which boosts their ability to think and execute," Brown says.

Create a list of priorities and use them to select which opportunities to pursue. "Don't be duped by the illusion of missed opportunity where you think you have to do everything that comes your way," Brown says. "Lock onto your goal and don't get distracted."

4. Work at the edge of your comfort zone.
Risk is necessary if you want to truly excel, and successful people approach risk with a clear sense of how much they can handle. "They take moderate risks," Brown says. "They're out of their comfort zone, but not going crazy."

Test your own boundaries by looking for risks that make you slightly uncomfortable, but still more excited than anxious. "You have an optimal risk range that you have to learn to gauge and understand," Brown says. "The more you experiment with taking risks, big and small, the easier it will be to find your sweet spot in the future."

5. Put your energy into the daily grind.
Successful people work tirelessly toward their goals. They're propelled by an internal energy that keeps them moving forward, even when they face setbacks or when success seems far away. "They keep giving to the process and keep investing," Brown says. "Their drive isn't pushy or demanding. It's persistent."

Rather than always looking ahead at the end goal, immerse yourself in the daily practice of building toward it. Learning to enjoy and embrace that process will help you develop the stamina and resilience you need to see it through.

According to Brown, "You should enjoy the pursuit of success. The chase lasts much longer than the catch."

As you continue to renew your thinking and take action toward your goals, you'll obtain and maintain your life transformation and success.

Conclusion

If you always think what you've always thought, you will always feel what you've always felt. If you always feel what you've always felt, you will always do what you've always done. If you always do what you've always done, you will always get what you always got. If you want a different result, you must change your MINDSET.

James Justin

Everything you need to transform your life and create the life of your dreams is in you! God has given you the power to transform your life!

You have the power to think, feel and free will. Use the power of your MIND to create and maintain an extraordinary life! Why settle for ordinary when your life can be extraordinary!

The process of transforming your life begins in your MIND. That's why I say, "If you change your MINDSET, you'll change your life!"

Your MINDSET is everything. Your MINDSET is your way of thinking. It's your belief system. It's your mental attitude. It determines your feelings, actions and results. As King Salomon said, "For as he thinks in his heart, so is he."

I wrote this book to help you transform your life. As you continue to practice the tips and strategies provided in this book, you'll be well in your way to maximizing your full potential and achieving your goals.

125

I encourage you to keep on developing yourself and pursuing your goals. As you continue to develop your thinking and pursue your goals, your life will be transformed!

In the words of Wilson Kanadi, *"To change your life, you have to change yourself. To change yourself, you have to change your MINDSET."* This book provides you with practical tools, tips and tactics you need to transform your life, and to achieve and maintain the life of your dreams. Now, it's your turn to take the next step toward the life of your dreams!

The Next Step

Are you ready to transform your life?

Are you wondering if you can really get going again, and transform your life from ordinary to extraordinary?

If so, you're not alone!

Many people are suffering, feeling afraid and being held back from achieving their full potential. I frequently hear these statements:

"I just want to be happier and to be myself."

"I know I'm just coasting along and I'm capable of a lot more."

"I feel like I'm stuck in a rut. I just want to feel like I belong and that people respect me."

"I'm NOT HAPPY!"

"I want to overcome my fear, but don't know how."

"Where are these self-doubts coming from?
I know I have some insecurities
and negative thoughts, but why?"

"I just want to live life on MY terms."

Breaking these thoughts and feelings are not as difficult as you may believe.

I wrote this book to help you achieve EXTRAORDINARY results!

I invite you to take the next step... "To change your MINDSET and change your life!" As you continue to practice the principles taught in this book, you'll be well on your way to transform your life! My clients and I have practiced the principles you just discovered in these pages, and the results have been remarkable. Now, it's your turn to take the next step to change your MINDSET and change your life!

If my clients achieved their goals, so can **YOU**!

Don't settle for an ordinary life, when you can achieve and enjoy an extraordinary life! Let's take the next step to transform your life!

You can get a great jump start with my introductory "New Beginnings" program. It's my gift to you, absolutely FREE! To get instant access to the "New Beginnings" MP3, visit CoachJamesJustin.com and sign up!

Notes

Justin MINDSET Survey

Name: _____

Date: _____

The goal of this survey is to help you identify the MINDSET controlling your life. Mindset is a particular way of thinking, a mental attitude or a belief system. Your mindset determines your feelings, your feelings determine your actions and your actions determine your results. If you change your mindset, you'll change your life!

Instructions:

Using the scale below, rate the following statements according to your level of agreement:

1 = Strongly Disagree
2 = Somewhat Disagree
3 = Not sure
4 = Somewhat Agree
5 = Strongly Agree

Questions:

1.   There's nothing I can do to make my life better.
    ___1 ___2 ___3 ___4 ___5

2. It is what it is. No matter what I try to do, nothing will ever change.
   ___1 ___2 ___3 ___4 ___5

3. Bad things always seem to happen to me, no matter what I try.
   ___1 ___2 ___3 ___4 ___5

4. Some people are just lucky in life.
   ___1 ___2 ___3 ___4 ___5

5. It's too late for me to change.
   ___1 ___2 ___3 ___4 ___5

6. I've always been like this.
   ___1 ___2 ___3 ___4 ___5

7. This is just the way I am.
   ___1 ___2 ___3 ___4 ___5

8. I've tried everything and nothing works.
   ___1 ___2 ___3 ___4 ___5

9. I believe success and happiness is a matter of luck.
   ___1 ___2 ___3 ___4 ___5

10. Let's be real, you are who you are, and that does not change.
    ___1 ___2 ___3 ___4 ___5

Add your total score from each question and write it down here: _____

What your score means

As we've discovered, there are two types of mindset.

People with the **fixed** MINDSET believe that their intelligence, skills and abilities are fixed; and their lives cannot be changed.

In contrast, people with the **growth** MINDSET believe that their lives can be transformed with new information, strategies and efforts.

Virtually, everyone who has achieved lasting success developed a growth mindset. If you want to transform your life and achieve lasting success, joy and happiness, I recommend that you adopt a growth mindset.

Here's what your score represents:

• **A score of 10–19** means that you have a growth MINDSET. You believe change is possible, and you're willing take action in that direction. You can benefit from coaching to help you develop a strategy to achieve your goals quicker.

• **A score of 20–29** means that you mostly have a growth MINDSET, but are still developing in that area. You also believe change is possible, but you procrastinate or find excuses not to take action in that direction. You can definitely benefit from coaching to help you overcome some of your fears and the obstacles preventing your success. A coach will hold you accountable to take action toward your goals.

• **A score of 30–39** means that you have mostly a fixed MINDSET, but need more work in developing a growth MINDSET. You've failed a few times and as a result doubt whether change is possible. You can definitely benefit from coaching to help you learn how to get back up again and empower yourself.

• **A score of 40–50** means that you have a fixed MINDSET. You believe your life will always be the way it is and there's nothing you can do to change it. You can also benefit from coaching to help you see your potential, and tap into your inner power.

Once you've identified your MINDSET, write 1-3 things that you're going to do to transform your life:

1. _____

2. _____

3. _____

To help you achieve extraordinary results, I'm offering a complimentary result coaching session! To get started, visit CoachJamesJustin.com and email me. I look forward to hearing from you today!

Values Assessment Worksheet

Name: _____

Date: _____

The goal of this assessment is to help you identify and document your core values. Core values are the things that matter to you the most.

Values Clarification Activities

1. Recall 1-3 events when you have been so absorbed in what you were doing that you did not even notice the time. What were you doing?

_____

_____

_____

2. What do you find meaningful in your life? This may include people, ideals, feelings and activities.

3. What values are most important to you? Circle all of the values that are most important to you from the following examples, and feel free to add your own:

- Achievements
- Advancement
- Autonomy

- Balance
- Group involvement
- Building something
- Challenge
- Compassion
- Competition
- Creativity
- Creating something
- Creating change
- Clarity
- Certainty
- Decision-making
- Entrepreneurship
- Equality
- Excitement/risk
- Fame
- Family happiness
- Financial security
- Friendships
- Fun
- Happiness
- Harmony
- Health
- Helping others
- Influencing people
- Improving something/perfecting something
- Independence
- Integrity
- Leadership
- Learning Gaining wisdom
- Leisure
- Listening
- Physical activity
- Being recognized/Impressing people

- Personal Growth
- Repairing something
- Respect
- Risk-taking
- Safety
- Security
- Self-expression
- Social belonging
- Serving others
- Spirituality
- Stability
- Status
- Teamwork
- Tenacity
- Visioning
- Wealth
- Other: _____

4 Benefits of Living Life According to Your Values

"Great people have great values and great ethics."
Jeffrey Gitomer

What are core values? One of the keys to a happier you is to identify your core values. More importantly, it's to live by your values.

As you embark on your extraordinary life journey, I want to encourage you to identify your values. Your values are the important things in your life. For example, I value my faith and spirituality; family and friends; fitness and health; fun and relaxation; and financial freedom.

Identifying your core values will give you the following benefits:

1. Focus and direction
2. Fewer disappointments
3. Greater self-awareness
4. More certainty and fulfillment

When you define your values, it will help you identify and prioritize what matters most to you in life. This process will help you plan ahead. It will also help you live life with a greater sense of awareness, certainty and fulfillment.

As you continue to live your life according to your values, you'll enjoy the benefits outlined in this book, and you'll be happier in life!

The Power of Your Subconscious Mind

Your subconscious mind is the powerhouse of your mental capabilities. It is the work desk of your mind. God has given you the power to think and to create the desire of your heart. The process of controlling and directing your subconscious mind is the key to personal transformation, healing and freedom.

Opportunities for unlimited abundance are all around you. There is an unlimited gold mine inside of you from which you can extract everything you need to create the life of your dreams. This is possible because you can think and take action to achieve your goals.

The process of controlling and directing your subconscious mind is the key to personal transformation.

You possess the gift to bring into your life more health, more wealth, more happiness and more success. God has given you the power to live life gloriously, joyously and abundantly. Jesus said, *"The thief comes only to steal and kill and destroy; I have come that they may have life, and have it to the full"* (John 10:10).

Because you have the gift to think and to take action, you can accomplish your heart's desires. As you continue to discover and release the power of your mind, you'll achieve extraordinary results.

The best way to release the power of your mind is to connect your thoughts and your feelings with the desired results. You can start by following these guidelines:

• Define your vision and goals.

• Commit to your strategy to achieve your goals. Use meditation, prayer, visualization and imagination to remain focused.

• Enlist the help of your team. Success is a team sport. Therefore, ask your team members to help you achieve your goals while you're helping them as well!

Besides short-term memory, the subconscious mind also plays an important role in our day-to-day functioning. It works hard at ensuring you have everything you need for quick recall and access to vital information when you need it, including the following:

Memories: This includes such things as your telephone number, driving a car without consciously thinking about it, and what you need to get from the store on your way home from work.

Current programs: These are the ones you run daily, such as behaviors, habits, mood filters, beliefs and values to process information and test its validity according to your perception of the world. This also includes intake from your five senses.

If your subconscious doesn't have a filter or reference point in its RAM for certain bits of information it receives, it has a direct line to the storage place of the mind: the unconscious. It will ask the unconscious to retrieve the programs it best associates with the incoming data to help make sense of it all.

The subconscious mind is also constantly at work, staying much more aware of your surroundings than you realize. In fact, according to the Neuro-linguistic programming (NLP) communication model, we are assaulted with more than 2 million bits of data every second. If your conscious mind had to crunch all that data, you would very quickly become overwhelmed and unable to accomplish much at all.

Instead, your subconscious mind filters out all the unnecessary information and delivers only that which is currently needed, in doses of around seven "chunks" at a time. It does all this "behind the scenes" so you can perform your daily work uninhibited. And it does this as logically as it can, based on the programs it can access in your unconscious mind.

The subconscious mind transmits all the results into consciousness via emotions, feelings, sensations, reflexes, images and dreams. It does not communicate in words.

The Link to the Subconscious Mind

One of the truly great things about the subconscious mind is that it obeys orders. This means that you can filter new information that supports your goals rather than focusing on what you don't want.

People often erroneously think that the **subconscious** mind is in charge and you are merely at its mercy.

In fact, it's the complete opposite. Your **conscious** mind gives it the direction–the favored environment–in which it operates.

The **subconscious** mind will only deliver the emotions and feelings of what you continuously think about. I am not saying it's as easy as changing what you think of in one moment, and your entire life will be changed overnight. There's usually a process to transform your thinking and your life. However, it can be done.

"Change happens when the pain of staying the same is greater than the pain of change."
Tony Robbins

The **unconscious** mind is very similar to the subconscious mind in that it also deals with memories. But there is a difference between the two.

Recall the triangle diagram, which describes the levels of the human mind. Remember that the unconscious mind sits a layer deeper in the mind, under the subconscious mind. Although the subconscious and unconscious minds have direct links to each other and deal with similar things, the unconscious mind is really the underground library of your memories, feelings, habits and behaviors.

The unconscious mind (the "hard drive of your memories), is the storehouse of all your deep-seated emotions that have been programmed since birth. These memories are usually programmed until the age of 12.

If you want significant change at a core level, this is where the real work begins…but it's not easy to locate!

You may need a professional counselor to help you recall some of your old memories that may be holding you back from achieving the life of your dreams. For additional help, visit CoachJamesJustin.com, and request a coaching session.

Unconscious versus Subconscious: What's the Difference?

There's been plenty of debate about whether the correct and more definitive term should be subconscious, or unconscious.

Unconscious is the term usually preferred by psychological professionals when referring to thoughts that are "out of reach" of our consciousness. Although they have similarities, it shouldn't be confused with the medical term for unconscious, which basically means "knocked out" or anesthetized.

The unconscious is the storage place for all our memories that have been repressed or that we don't wish to recall. The blocked memory of a traumatic childhood event is an example, but it doesn't have to be as serious as that. It could be something very distant such as what you had for lunch on your first day of school, or the name of a childhood friend you seldom played with.

It is a memory that we can't retrieve at our choosing. It's there, but we can't remember it no matter how hard we try. Certain psychoanalytical methods such as hypnosis can recall these memories, or it can be triggered by a particular event, scent or environment.

We are unable to recall anything in our unconscious without it being triggered by some special event or technique.

The important point to remember here is that we cannot remember anything in our unconscious without it being triggered by some special event or technique. This is how the unconscious works.

The subconscious on the other hand, is similar, except that it enables us to choose to remember. The memories are closer to the conscious surface, and thus more easily accessible with a little focus.

For example, if I asked you for your phone number, you could easily bring that into conscious thought. The interesting thing is that before I asked you to recall it, you had no conscious thought of your phone number. It was stored in your subconscious, available for ready recall when needed.

This further illustrates how your subconscious resembles computer RAM, in that they both keep the chunks of information you most often use, close to the surface and easy to remember.

If, however, recalling your phone number isn't important to you, that information may then be stored a bit deeper, making it more difficult to recall at a later time.

The Role of the Unconscious

In many respects the unconscious deals with all the same tasks as the subconscious: memory, habits, feelings, emotions and behaviors. The difference between the two minds, however, is that your unconscious mind is the source of all the programs that your subconscious uses.

It stores all your memories and experiences since birth. It's from these memories that your beliefs, habits and behaviors are formed and reinforced over time. It's where dreams are experienced when you are asleep. This part of your mind is responsible for attracting pleasure and avoiding pain as much as possible.

As you continue to discover the power of your mind and take action toward your goals, your life will be transformed!

The Sound Mind Prayer

Heavenly Father, I surrender my mind to you. I consent to the truth that is found in your word and in your word alone. Today, I chose to be transformed by the renewing of my mind.

Day by day fill my thought life with images of who you are. I pray that out of your glorious riches you may strengthen me with power through your Spirit, so that Christ may dwell in my heart through faith.

And I pray that being rooted and established in love; I may have power to grasp how wide and long and high and deep is your love for me. I want to grow in this love that surpasses knowledge—that I may be filled to the measure of all the fullness of God each day.

Empower me today to guard my mind and to aim it toward heavenly things. I call upon your divine power to demolish the strongholds in my life. I demolish all arguments and every pretension that sets itself up against the knowledge of God, and I take captive every thought, every feeling and every action to make them obedient to Christ.

I now go forward filled with God's power, love and a sound mind!

Dr. Lauretta Justin

5 Steps to Attract Abundance

"The thief comes only to steal and kill and destroy. I came that you may have life and have it abundantly."
John 10:10

The abundant life is available to you! And since everything you need to attract unlimited abundance is already inside you, if you discover how to attract it, you'll have it forever.

Everyone has their own definition for abundance. That's why it's best to create your own definition.
The abundant life includes both the science of achievement and the art of finding meaning and fulfillment.

Step 1: Clearly define the desires of your heart, and seek God's wisdom and professional help to turn your desires into reality.

"Delight yourself in the Lord, and he will give you the desires of your heart."
Psalm 37:4

Step 2: Change your MINDSET, change your life!

"See the world as an abundant, providing, friendly place. When you change the way you look at things, the things you look at change. When you see the world as abundant and friendly your intentions are genuine possibilities"
Dr. Wayne Dyer

145

Step 3: Meditate on who you are and what you want. We often waste too much energy and resources on what we don't want. Instead, I encourage you to focus on your goals and who you are. For example, you can affirm the following:

"I am a child of God; and I have the mind of Christ. I'm attracting all my blessings!"

"I attract success and abundance into my life and my business because that is who I am."

"Whatever things are true, whatever things are noble, whatever things are just, whatever things are pure, whatever things are lovely, whatever things are of good report, if there is any virtue and if there is anything praiseworthy—meditate on these things."
Philippians 4:8

Step 4: Take actions that support your thoughts and feelings of abundance and success.
Plan your strategy. But remember that a plan without action is no plan at all. Therefore, if you want to attract unlimited abundance, I encourage you to take positive actions that support your goals.

Step 5: Live to Give. Develop and maintain an attitude of giving and helping others. When you give, you open your heart to receive.
When you help others, you give a loan to God; and God never leaves a debt unpaid. As you continue to practice these steps, you'll position yourself to attract abundance in your life!

10 Tips to Overcome Fear

"One of the greatest discoveries a man makes, one of his great surprises, is to find he can do what he was afraid he couldn't do."
Henry Ford

We all have fear. Fear in small doses is healthy. It warns us of danger and keeps us in check. It helps us to show respect and honor to our parents and other authorities.

However, when fear goes unchecked, a HUGE part of our emotional intelligence suffers. We get stuck. We get unhappy. Don't let fear stop you from achieving the life of your dreams.

1. Acknowledge your fear, don't deny it.

2. Analyze your fear to determine its source.

3. Determine if your fear is legitimate by categorizing it as either rational or irrational.

4. If the fear is rational and it serves a crucial purpose, keep it. However, if it's irrational, make a plan to confront it and overcome it.

5. Get help! Find a professional Life Coach who can help you.

6. Become curious about what you're afraid of, and learn as much as you can about it.

147

7. Take slow breaths at the initial feeling of fear.

8. Sleep and eat well-balanced meals.

9. Exercise regularly to change your mental state.

10.   Seek guidance, and connect with loving people who can help you.

For more tips on how to overcome your fears, visit CoachJamesJustin.com and request a complementary coaching session today!

3 Tips to transform your life this year

Imagine having the right strategies, the tools, the support and the guidance you need to achieve your goals this year!

How would it feel to know that you're running at your optimum level, achieving extraordinary results, and experiencing greater success, joy and HAPPINESS?

You can get a great jump-start right now with our "New Beginnings" Coaching program. It's my gift to you, absolutely FREE! The "New Beginnings" program features people like you! It highlights success stories of our clients; where they were, what was holding them back and where they are now.

Using the Justin's Life Coaching, they achieved some incredible transformational results!

Let's make THIS YEAR the best one ever! Let's think and dream bigger dreams, plan bigger outcomes, take action in a bigger way, and experience a ton of success, joy, happiness, personal accomplishment and professional fulfillment!

1) Get a Life Coach in your corner. Successful and happy people always enlist the help of others who can help them achieve their goals.

2) Commit to ongoing growth and development. Attend educational webinars, workshops and conferences. People who are very successful and happy participate in ongoing learning activities to improve and increase their knowledge and wisdom.

3) Celebrate your wins! Big or small, you must celebrate every milestone toward your goal. This will keep you encouraged and motivated to move forward.

Everything you need to create the life you want is at your disposal. You just have to take the first step.

I know you can do it!

YOU know you can do it! So…let's just do it!

Contact us for coaching and get the help you need to achieve your goals.

7 Tips to Improve your Self-Esteem

Self-esteem is an overall assessment of your worth. It's about accepting and appreciating yourself for who you are, including your entire personhood…the strong you and the weak you.

Don't let low self-esteem prevent you from achieving and enjoying the life of your dreams.

"Low self-esteem is like internal bleeding. You look normal on the outside but are dying inside."
Dr. Lauretta Justin

1. Identify your strengths and weaknesses. Take a self-inventory survey.

2. Acknowledge that you are not perfect. Decide to maximize your strengths and get help in the areas that you are weak in.

3. Develop a positive MINDSET through positive affirmations, prayers and meditations.

4. Assemble a professional team including a counselor or a coach to help you define your vision, purpose, passion and goals.

5. Develop a smart strategy to transform your life.

6. Take 1 step per day to achieve your goals.

7. Celebrate each progressive step you make toward the life of your dreams, and enjoy everyday life with your loved ones.

Improving your self-esteem is an ongoing process. And it is a process that is unique to each person. It takes love, support and commitment.

You don't have to pursue this goal alone. We are here to help you!

For coaching to achieve extraordinary results, visit CoachJamesJustin.com!

3 Tips to Boost Your Confidence

"With realization of one's own potential and self-confidence in one's ability, one can build a better world."
Dalai Lama

Self-confidence is one of the keys to greater success and happiness. Your confidence begins in your mind. It empowers you to perform your skills and abilities more efficiently. Your confidence is developed by believing and practicing what you are great at doing.

Confidence is a feeling and a belief that you can do something well, or succeed at a goal. People with high self-confidence believe in their knowledge, abilities and skills, and use their resources to achieve defined goals. When you believe in yourself, you'll have the confidence to set, to pursue and to achieve your goals.

Here are the 3 Tips to boost your confidence:

1. Stop comparing yourself.
• You're unique and you're special!
• Love and accept yourself if you want to gain the confidence required to achieve your goals.
• "Be yourself. Everyone else is already taken" (Oscar Wilde).

2. Relax, you're not alone.
• We all have low self-confidence in some area in our lives.
• Identify the area you want to improve.
• Get the help you need to master it.

• **Never stop developing and growing.** The path to success requires continue growth.

3. Do what you love.
• Life is too short to waste your precious time, money and energy on meaningless activities. Invest your time and energy into the things that bring you the greatest returns.
• Take one step per day toward achieving and enjoying what you love in your life.
• Share and help others do the same. When you help and share constructively, it builds confidence and significance.

The good news is that we all can boost our self-confidence! It does not matter how low our confidence may be right now...we can always improve it. It's a matter of making the choice and following the simple steps outlined in this book. I hope that you will take the necessary time and effort to improve yourself and enjoy life to its fullest!

The Key to a Happier You

Imagine for a moment, the happiest people you know. What images appear?

They're probably smiling, laughing and willingly greeting you.

There are those people who always seem to be happy...no matter what! They are happy in good times, and they are even able to find happiness in the bad times.

What's their secret?

Were they born with a happiness gene? Are they simply lucky? Is there something wrong with them?

It's actually simpler than that.

Rather than a happiness gene, the secret comes from their perspective. They simply choose to see the silver lining in every cloud. And YOU have the power to make that same choice!

Perspective is EVERYTHING! And it's the key to your happiness if you know how it works! Happy people make the choice to be happy, and practice it regularly. If they can do it, so can you! For more tips on happiness, or for personal and professional coaching, visit CoachJamesJuston.com.

How to Achieve Your Goals Quickly

Successful people create goals, and take actions to achieve them.

The KFC Principles of Success

Around the world, Kentucky Fried Chicken (KFC) is known as one of the most recognizable brands in the restaurant industry. Beside McDonald's, KFC is the second-largest food chain in the world. Every year over a billion KFC chicken dinners are served. We can all thank Harland "Colonel" Sanders for his vision and his relentless efforts to develop the KFC brand. He founded KFC in 1930 in North Corbin, Kentucky, and in 1952 he launched the first KFC franchise in Salt Lake City, Utah.

To achieve his goals, Colonel Sanders followed certain proven strategies that have become even more effective over time.

1. **K**now exactly what you want and write it down. When you write down a specific goal, it becomes established. It is easier to express it and get people to help you.

2. **F**ind out your current status. Before you make any significant changes in your life and in your business, you must know where you are and where you want to be. Once you identify your current status, develop 1-3 actions you will take to get what you want…and then just do it!

3. **C**hange your MINDSET to support your goals. Our MINDSETs affect everything about ourselves. What you

want is to have a growth MINDSET that supports your goals. You can start by getting new information that is consistent with what you want.

Whatever you hold in your mind will tend to occur in your life. If you continue to believe as you have always believed, you will continue to act as you have always acted. If you continue to act as you have always acted, you will continue to get what you have always gotten. If you want different results in your life or your work, all you have to do is change your mind and pursue your goals!

We all need help sometime to achieve our goals. If you need help, ASK!

Are you ready to transform your life and your business?

Get started now by visiting CoachJamesJustin.com, and email us!

How to Create Lasting Change

Every year, many people make resolutions to achieve certain goals. It might be during the beginning of a new year or on their birthday each year. At the time of writing the resolutions, most people feel very confident about reaching those goals. However, only about 8% of people actually achieve their New Year's resolutions goals, according to Forbes.com. That means a whopping 92% of people fail to achieve their goals!

3 Tips to Create Lasting Changes

• Break down the process into 3-5 simple steps. I highly recommend starting with only 3 steps. In this case, less is better.

• These steps must reflect things that you are either already doing, have done successfully in the past or things you know you can do. You must feel confident that you can do each one of these steps comfortably.

• Find a way to put those steps into automation, and then forget about it. Before you know it, you will have reached your goals. To automate your new change, you must repeat it over and over until it becomes conditioned and first nature.

Creating Your Own Opportunities

"Opportunity is missed by most people because it is dressed in overalls, and looks like work."
Thomas Edison

Opportunities to succeed are all around us! Here are 5 Steps to attract opportunities to you **RIGHT NOW!**

1. Have an attitude of gratitude.

2. Learn from your failures and keep trying.

3. Don't be afraid of new ideas; be willing to try new things.

4. Hang around successful people.

5. Get in the habit of giving more than what is expected.

Procrastination

"Procrastination is one of the most common and deadliest of diseases, and its toll on success and happiness is heavy."
Wayne Gretzky

Procrastination is to delay doing something until a later time because you do not want to do it. When you put things off until a later time, you will increase your stress and decrease your success. Here are 7 steps to overcome procrastination:

- Make a list of all projects or tasks.

- Break down big projects into small pieces.

- Prioritize the list in the order of importance and due dates.

- Delegate tasks by those that must be completed by you, and those that can be done by others.

- Ask for help! Delegate other tasks to other team members.

- Get a timer and commit 20 minutes of focus each day to complete a task toward the goal.

- Utilize an accountability partner and report progress as agreed.

One of the best ways to use these tips and overcome procrastination is to enlist the resources of your team to keep you accountable.

More Inspirational Quotes on MINDSET

"Your mind is like a muscle; the more you use it, the stronger it gets."
James Justin

"We can complain because rose bushes have thorns, or rejoice because thorn bushes have roses."
Abraham Lincoln

"If you have a dream, don't just sit there; gather courage to believe that you can succeed and leave no stone unturned to make it a reality."
Dr. Roopleen

"If you have a positive attitude and constantly strive to give your best effort, eventually you will overcome your immediate problems and find you are ready for greater challenges."
Pat Riley

"Believe in yourself! Have faith in your abilities! Without a humble but reasonable confidence in your own powers, you cannot be successful or happy."
Norman Vincent Peale

References

1. THE HOLY BIBLE. (1982). New King James Version (NKJV). Nashville, TN: Thomas Nelson, Inc.

2. Justin, J. (2016). MINDSET: HOW TO TRANSFORM YOUR LIFE FROM ORDINARY TO EXTRAORDINARY. Freedom Living International: Orlando, FL.

3. Dweck, C. (2007). MINDSET: THE NEW PSYCHOLOGY OF SUCCESS. Ballantine Books: New York City, New York.

4. Meyer, J. (2012). POWER THOUGHTS: 12 STRATEGIES TO WIN THE BATTLE OF THE MIND. Faithwords: Nashville, Tennessee.

5. Meyer, J. (2005). BATTLEFIELD OF THE MIND DEVOTIONAL: 100 INSIGHTS THAT WILL CHANGE THE WAY YOU THINK. Faithwords: Nashville, Tennessee.

6. Smith, B. (2016). MINDSET: HOW POSITIVE THINKING WILL SET YOU FREE & HELP YOU ACHIEVE MASSIVE SUCCESS IN LIFE. CreateSpace Independent Publishing Platform: North Charleston, SC.

7. Maltz, M. (1989). PSYCHO-CYBERNETICS: A NEW WAY TO GET MORE LIVING OUT OF LIFE. Chicago, IL: Pocket Books.

8. Siebold, S. (2010). 177 MENTAL TOUGHNESS SECRETS OF THE WORLD CLASS: THE THOUGHT

PROCESSES, HABITS AND PHILOSOPHIES OF THE GREAT ONES, 3RD EDITION. London House Press: Montgomery County, Ohio.

9.   Coué, É. (2011). SELF-MASTERY THROUGH CONSCIOUS AUTOSUGGESTION. Space Independent Publishing Platform: Mustang, OK.

10.   Stoop, D. (2003). YOU ARE WHAT YOU THINK. Ada, MI: Revell Publishing.

11.   Schwartz, D.J. (2015). THE MAGIC OF THINKING BIG. Chicago, IL: Touchstone.

12.   Cloud, H. (1993). CHANGES THAT HEAL. Grand Rapids, Michigan: Zondervan.

13.   Davis, L. R. (2014). NEGATIVE SELF TALK (4 book series). CreateSpace Independent Publishing Platform: North Charleston, SC. ISBN-13: 978-1499385601.

14.   Hill, N. (2015). Think and Grow Rich: The keys to a successful prosperous life. Kindle Edition. ASIN: B00U0FR1RA.

15.   Rohn, J. (1996). 7 Strategies for Wealth & Happiness: Power Ideas from America's Foremost Business Philosopher. Harmony Books: NYC, NY. ISBN-13: 978-0761506164.

About the Author

A born leader, James Justin hasn't let any obstacles stand in his way. And he has the skills to make sure *your* obstacles are broken and no longer stand in your way.

"It's my passion to inspire and help you transform, optimize and accelerate your life! This passion led me to earn my master's degree in the field of counseling, and dedicate my life to speaking, coaching and helping people like YOU for over 20 years!"

James Justin is an entrepreneur, ordained minister, speaker, author and life coach. He earned his Master's of Social Work (MSW) degree from Boston College, and his Bachelor of Social Work (BSW) degree from Eastern Nazarene College in Quincy, Massachusetts.

In 2011, James and his wife, Dr. Lauretta, co-authored and published their first book, "Express Yourself!" In 2013, James published his solo book project titled "How to Develop Healthy Relationships with Anyone!" Both titles are available on his website or wherever books are sold.

James also worked as a professional counselor for the state of Florida for more than seven years prior to pursuing his passion and his dream: to help people, and make an impact in the private sector.

James married his high school sweetheart, Dr. Lauretta Justin, and they are the proud parents of three incredible and very active boys.

The Justins spend the majority of their free time focusing on "the boys" (in other words, trying to keep up with them)! James enjoys reading, writing and hanging out with family and friends.

James is committed to helping create transformational growth with each and every one of his clients. And he's available to help you achieve extraordinary results. To contact James, visit CoachJamesJustin.com!

Products

You can get our products at CoachJamesJustin.com and on Amazon!

Books & eBooks:

1. MINDSET: How to Transform Your Life from Ordinary to Extraordinary by James Justin

2. 7 Days to a Happier You by James Justin

3. 12 Tips to Achieve Financial Freedom: The Simple Guide to Successfully Manage your Personal Finances by James Justin

4. 7 Steps to Develop Healthy Relationships with Anyone by James Justin

5. Positive Parenting: 12 Tips to Prepare Your Kids for Success by James Justin

6. Parenting Digital Natives: What Parents Can Do About the Danger of Social Media and Online Activities of Their Kids by Dr. Lauretta Justin

7. Christian Counseling by James Justin and Dr. Lauretta Justin

8. The Power of Prayer by James Justin and Dr. Lauretta Justin

9. Yes, You Can! How You Can Overcome "The Seven Dream Killers" to Get the Life of Your Dreams by Dr. Lauretta Justin

10. CEO OF YOU: How to Create the Business and the Life of Your Dreams by Dr. Lauretta Justin

11. Hero by Nathan Justin

Music CD:

1. The Spirit of Christmas by Dr. Lauretta Justin

Book Description

"MINDSET is everything... It determines your Feelings, your feelings determine your Actions, and your actions determine your Results. If you change your MINDSET, you'll change your life!"

—James Justin

Everything you need to succeed is already within you. All this book does is helping you automate it by helping you change your limiting beliefs. This MINDSET playbook features success stories from people like you who have used its' principles to achieve extraordinary results!

It's a step-by-step playbook, taking you on a journey to transform your life and accelerate your path to extraordinary results. No matter your stage of life, or when you started, this book will provide you the tools and the help needed to achieve your goals more rapidly than you ever thought possible.

It's not what you don't know that's limiting your success; it's what you don't know that you don't know. Your MINDSET holds the key to the abundant life. Playbook is written to help you maximize your full potential; and to achieve lasting success, joy and happiness!

Are you ready to have mind-blowing success? If so, you're invited to take the journey into MINDSET!

WHAT LEADERS ARE SAYING ABOUT MINDSET:

"This book is a must-read if you want to reach your full potential and achieve lasting success and happiness. It offers simple yet practical steps to accomplish any goal."
—Dr. Lauretta Justin, Optometrist, Speaker & Author of 'Yes You Can!'

"At a time when I considered myself 'un-coachable,' I got so stuck and frustrated with my stalled career that I felt like giving up...and couldn't even really figure out how to get unstuck and succeed! A friend insisted I read **MINDSET***; and I'm glad I did! James Justin skillfully walks the reader through his proven and simple path to transform your life. When I realized how to change my* **MINDSET***, as well as to begin asking the right questions and pursue my goals, my life transformed; and it has never been the same!" If you're ready to transform your life and your business, get this book and implement James Justin's principles for success."*
—Mark Wahlton, Freelance Journalist & Editor

www.ingramcontent.com/pod-product-compliance
Lightning Source LLC
Chambersburg PA
CBHW072007090426
42740CB00011B/2124